Massey on Money

DAVID
&
NORA,

BEST WISHES!

Jeff

DAVID
x
YOOY
MIZHEZ.
R739

HOW TO PLAN, PROTECT AND
MAKE YOUR MONEY LAST FOR LIFE!

YOUR GUIDE TO RETIREMENT

Massey

on

Money™

RADIO SHOW HOST

JEFFREY H. MASSEY
CERTIFIED FINANCIAL PLANNER™

BRIGHTSTAR PUBLISHING

MASSEY ON MONEY

How to Plan, Protect and Make Your Money Last for Life!

ISBN   978-1-61961-758-2 *Paperback*

978-1-61961-759-9 *Ebook*

DISCLOSURE

Contents

Introduction

A few years ago, two of my clients came into my office. They were a married couple. Let's call them John and Suzanne. John was worried that he would not be able to retire, and he was pretty worked up about it. At seventy years old, he'd worked all his life and was still working. His wife, Suzanne, was hoping John could retire someday and not have to get up early and go to work every single day. They both wanted to be able to enjoy themselves in their retirement.

When I have clients in this type of situation (preparing to retire), I will typically begin to build a retirement income plan for them. To establish a solid foundation for a retirement income plan, I begin with these questions:

- How much money do you need to retire?

- What are your day-to-day living costs?
- What are your other lifestyle expenses?

From there, I'll determine what income is needed in retirement, subtract the expected income, and determine if there will be a shortage. If there is an expected income from social security or a pension fund, I'll apply that toward the income projection. After I have that information, I'll perform an analysis and develop an income plan designed to last throughout their lifetime.

Everyone has different needs based on their unique situation. We remind people of this quite often on our weekly radio show *Massey on Money*. Many people listen to the show, and we're grateful for that. I've been giving out helpful tips and strategies on the radio since 2006, and I've been helping people with their financial matters since 1987.

ONE COMMON FEAR AMONG RETIREES

In the surveys I've read about retirees, their number-one fear is running out of money. People fear running out of money more than they fear death. Having enough money to last throughout retirement is the primary concern of the people I meet with, whether they've saved $200,000 or $2 million for retirement.

I recently met with a client who had over $1.5 million in

investments and savings. He was retired, and his wife was working part time. They could easily replace her income with income from their investments, and they could certainly afford to retire. I was surprised to find out that even these two were concerned about running out of money. They had over $1 million in liquid investments, yet they had the same fear.

Many people I work with have the dollars saved and put aside, but they don't know how to convert those saved dollars into a lifetime income plan. That's my focus, and I show my clients how to structure an income that is designed to last as long as they do.

THE BENEFITS OF PROFESSIONAL GUIDANCE

In my opinion, it's important to work with a professional who does this type of retirement planning every day. This is most likely the first time you've retired, but it's not my first time. As a retirement planner, I've essentially retired hundreds of times with my clients.

When you go on vacation, you can try to figure out everything yourself. You can research what you want to see and do, and manage the logistics and scheduling of your itinerary. However, if you hire a tour guide, you can be much more efficient. The tour guide knows the places you should go and the places you should avoid. The guide knows the best times to go, and knows how to keep you out of trouble.

As fiduciary advisors, that is exactly what we do for your retirement planning. We are retirement tour guide specialists. Our goal is to guide you through your retirement years, to help you avoid hitting as many bumps in the road as possible.

The best reward for me comes when I present my clients with their retirement plan. It's extremely fulfilling to see the confidence people feel when they realize they now have a plan to help them pursue the retirement lifestyle they deserve. That's one aspect I truly love as I guide people into and through their retirement years.

HOW MY PARENTS' STRUGGLE IMPACTED ME

When meeting with clients, I often think of my own parents and childhood. I was one of six children, and my dad was a factory worker. He worked three jobs to keep the family afloat. We were a poor family, but my dad was too proud to accept any type of financial assistance. I was the third son, so I had to wear all kinds of hand-me-downs. I would leave the house with torn jeans, which embarrassed my mother. She would cry if any of us left the house wearing pants with a hole, because it showed others we were poor.

In the fifth grade, my mom would make my lunch and put it in a brown paper bag. On my way to school, I would unwrap it and take a peek at what I had for lunch. All too often, it was a mayonnaise sandwich. There was no bologna and no ham. It was just mayonnaise and bread. This would continue to happen occasionally, even into my high school years.

When I was fifteen years old, my dad came to me with an offer. "Are you looking for some spending money?" he asked me.

"Oh yeah!" I said. "Are you going to give me an allowance?" None of my four older siblings had ever received an allowance, so I was quite surprised by the possibility of getting one.

"No," my dad said. "Your uncle needs someone to wash dishes at his restaurant. You'll have to ride your bicycle three miles to get there and three miles to get back home. Also, the rule in our house is that you give half of your paycheck to your mother."

I accepted the job. Every Saturday, I rode my bicycle three miles to my job, worked for seven hours, and earned fourteen dollars. Then I rode my bicycle three miles back home, where I had to give my mother seven dollars. By the time I was a senior in high school, I was working part time, which was thirty-nine hours per week. As a teenager, I was essentially paying for room and board, and doing so at the rate of thirty-five dollars per week. In today's dollars, this would be the equivalent of a teenager giving his parents $289 a week, and I did that all the way through high school.

My dad always wanted to retire at fifty-five years old. He was able to leave the factory at that age, but he couldn't retire. He still needed income. To earn money, he started collecting newspapers. When we were very young, my brothers and I would help him. We would knock on people's front doors and ask if they had newspapers we could take for them. We would collect newspapers in a huge, ten-foot-long box truck. When the truck was full, we would then sell the newspapers to a recycling plant. That was our typical Saturday: four boys riding on a truck with our dad, knocking on doors to ask for newspapers.

In addition to collecting newspapers, my dad was able to build up a lawn-mowing business after he'd left the factory. At the age of sixty-nine, he had a triple-bypass heart surgery. That slowed him down a bit, but he kept working. There was just no way he could afford to quit.

Because of my parents' financial struggles, I had a twisted view about money for a long time. I focused entirely on attracting money, working for money, and saving money.

I saw my dad work tirelessly, and I did the same thing. I always had my primary job, and another part-time job.

For example, I saved enough money to buy a rental property. I would come home from my job, have dinner, and go work on the rental property. I would go to bed late at night only to get up at six o'clock the next morning to do it all over again. I did that for many years because of my view about money and finances.

I want my clients to be in a better position. I don't want my clients to be worried about their finances and money. As my clients get closer to retirement, we create a plan to take care of their retirement income needs. They can feel relieved and comfortable with the plan we put together, and confident that their plan was designed to provide income for as long as they are alive.

THE IMPORTANCE OF PLANNING AND PROTECTING

Many years ago, many people could survive on their social security income, but things have changed dramatically. Social security was never intended to be the sole source of income for retirement, but for many decades, people could actually survive on it. As things have become more expensive, however, you can't rely on social security checks as your only income during retirement. Historically, social security checks have not kept up with the real pace of inflation for retirees.

Inflation has changed life as we know it. I paid $32,000 for my first house, and now, many *cars* cost more than that. According to a Kelley Blue Book report from April 2015, the average price of a new car is $33,560.[1]

I mentioned how thirty-five dollars during my high school years is now the equivalent of $289. That's a big difference. It's important to put money aside as early as possible so you'll be in a good position to overcome the obstacles of increased costs.

As you near retirement, you might also consider changing financial advisors. Advisors tend to have a niche and a bias. My niche is retirement income planning and conservative investment. My bias is to preserve money. My primary goal is to preserve each client's money, and my secondary goal is to structure a plan to make that money last throughout retirement.

A stockbroker-type of advisor will try to grow your money, but won't necessarily build an overall retirement income plan. They might tell you about an individual stock they

---

1 "New Car Transaction Prices Rise Steadily, Up 2.6 Percent in April 2015, According to Kelley Blue Book," Kelley Blue Book, May 1, 2015, https://mediaroom.kbb.com/2015-05-01-New-Car-Transaction-Prices-Rise-Steadily-Up-2-6-Percent-in-April-2015-According-to-Kelley-Blue-Book.

think you should buy, but that's where their advising typically ends. At Massey & Associates, Inc., however, we build an entire plan for each client's retirement.

If you're five or ten years away from retiring, we can help you structure your portfolio so you won't have to give up large chunks of your savings just before you retire, in the event of a stock market crash similar in magnitude to the crash that occurred in 2008. We achieve this restructuring by adjusting the risk level of your investments based on what we discover when conducting something we call a "stress test." In a stress test, we'll show you what could happen to your portfolio if the economy takes a negative turn.

For instance, if the economic meltdown of 2008 were to happen again, how would that impact your current investments? We can answer that question with our analysis. We can do the same type of analysis for over fifty different scenarios, such as:

- What if interest rates go up?
- What if the stock market goes down dramatically, like it did in 2008?
- What if China continues to slow down?
- What if nothing gets done and everything stalemates in Washington, DC?

Based on that analysis, we look at a client's portfolio and

see if their current plan is structured in an acceptable way. Sadly, many people we meet with are carrying too much risk in their portfolios as they near their retirement years. When you walk through the door of retirement, you want to make sure your plan is in place and your income will be there.

CHALLENGES FOR CURRENT INVESTORS

There weren't many stock market investment options available to the average investor until IRAs came out in 1974[2] and 401(k)s were created in 1978.[3] At that point, the door was opened for the average worker to invest their money directly into the stock market.

That changed everything. Ultimately, the risks and responsibilities of investing were forced onto the shoulders of each individual employee. That was problematic because the average worker didn't know how to avoid the pitfalls of investing. How do you analyze a stock? How do you know the difference between a good stock and a bad stock? How do you know which mutual funds are the best?

In previous generations, employees were given pensions. It was the responsibility of the company you worked for

---

2   "Individual Retirement Account," Wikipedia, https://en.wikipedia.org/wiki/Individual_retirement_account

3   "401k," Wikipedia, https://en.wikipedia.org/wiki/401(k).

to ensure there was enough money in the pension fund. However, with the advent of 401(k)s, the risks and responsibilities of investing transitioned onto the shoulders of each individual employee.

Sadly, the average person doesn't understand the financial world. It's not what most people do in their daily work, and our education system does not adequately train people on financial issues. That's one of my pet peeves. I'm currently a member of the Financial Planning Association of Rhode Island, an organization I have also served as president and chairman, and part of our mission is to teach people about financial topics.

This book has the same mission. I want to help you become more educated about your finances, because you're typically not taught about this in school. You need to rely on a financial professional, and I believe it's best to work with someone who has attained the Certified Financial Planner™ (CFP®) designation. The CFP® designation is the highest financial planning designation that can be earned, and it is an internationally recognized certification. Why would you work with somebody who's not at that level?

BENEFITS OF STARTING EARLY AND STAYING INVESTED

As with anything in life, the earlier you get started, the

better the outcome should be. There are so many different things to think about relative to your finances. Reach back and pat yourself on the back, because reading this book is a great step toward educating yourself about your finances. Not everybody takes the time to educate themselves on their own finances, and many people I meet with have no idea what they have in their investment accounts.

When the stock market tanked in 2008, many people showed up in my office for a complimentary consultation with several months of bank statements *still sealed in the envelopes*. People weren't even opening their statements! They were afraid of what they'd see inside.

The good news was that they were ten or more years away from retirement and they were still saving money toward retirement. That's the important part. It can benefit you to continue your contributions during bad times in the market. Let's say you bought a stock for ten dollars per share, and the next month the share price sinks to nine dollars. For the same ten dollars you spent in the prior month, you can now buy more shares. You're building up more shares of stock, and when the stock recovers, you have more shares to recover with. Your recovery could then happen more quickly because you continued investing.

You can have an advantage over the long run if you continue your investment contributions while things are a little dicey in the markets. The average person may not know that, but that's the kind of advice you can get from a financial advisor.

WHAT'S AT STAKE

As you get closer to retirement, it becomes critical to circle the wagons around your money and preserve what you have saved. Having your money fully at risk in the stock market could result in losing up to 40 percent of your retirement money if there's a stock market collapse like the one we experienced in 2008. You could be less than a year away from retiring, but if heavy losses occur, you may need to keep working for several more years to rebuild your assets.

It gets worse when you consider the reality that you may not still have a job in the event of another economic collapse. Many people in 2008 and 2009 lost both their savings and their jobs. They lost their money first because they were positioned with too much risk in the market when it tanked. Then, they lost their jobs because their companies closed or downsized. It was a double whammy.

It's absolutely critical to protect a higher percentage of your investments as you near retirement so you're not left holding the bag after a stock market decline. After all, you don't want to end up eating a mayonnaise sandwich!

HOW WE CAN HELP

At Massey & Associates, Inc., our goal is to be the retirement tour guide who helps you through the process, showing you how to preserve and protect your assets and avoid the potential pitfalls. We use a combination of stock market investments and insurance-based products. Only insurance-based products can provide you with an income that you cannot outlive, and those types of products are called annuities.

The first step is to analyze where you are right now. We take each of our clients through the process of analyzing their current financial situation. We learn the level of risk contained in a client's current investments, and we learn the risk level acceptable to each client. We want to know all of the details, and this analysis becomes our basis for the second step.

After we know exactly where you are financially, we can then analyze areas that are weak, and suggest some better alternatives. We will lay out a plan, piece by piece, and explain how to spread your assets into as many "buckets" as necessary to accomplish your retirement income goals. When you're ready to walk through that door into retirement, we'll have a plan and will begin to implement it.

Most of our clients utilize a combination of investments and insurance-based products. It's important to work with an advisor who has access to both types of products. When you work with an advisor who only sells insurance products, it's like going into the boxing ring with one hand tied behind your back. Similarly, if you work with a stockbroker, they're only going to invest in stocks and bonds. In either scenario, dealing with advisors who focus on only one type of product or investment means you are fighting with one hand tied behind your back. Wouldn't you rather fight with both hands?

We are fiduciary advisors, which means we work in the best interest of our clients. We bring our clients solutions that we feel are the best fit for their needs. This may be an insurance product, an investment, or some combination of the two. As I mentioned earlier, I have a bias to protect assets and avoid big losses. To do that, you often need a combination of insurance products and investments.

Typical investment salespeople often believe that it's safer to invest in bonds. They believe people should invest in bonds for their safety position. Bonds, however, are not a true safety position. In Rhode Island, when the city of Central Falls went bankrupt, bondholders lost money. Puerto Rico is currently in an awful situation, and many of their bondholders will likely lose money. Detroit and several other municipalities have also declared bankruptcy in the past. Individuals holding municipal bonds in those cities were greatly hurt.

We work with true safety positions and balance that safety with growth opportunities in the stock market. As complete financial advisors, we bring it all together and build a structure that you can see and understand. Our clients give us positive feedback, saying that they can finally understand their financial plan and how it works.

THE ADVANTAGE OF EXPERT TEAMS

In addition to the advisory team within our office, we also work with two organizations that give us detailed analyses of insurance products and investments. Using that analysis, we're able to show you the overall level of risk and the exact fees you're paying.

We provide investment advisory services through AE Wealth Management, LLC. Advisors Excel, the nation's largest independent marketing organization, helps us analyze insurance-based products underwritten by more than fifty different companies.

As fiduciary advisors, we work in our clients' best interest. After we've conducted our analysis to determine our clients' needs, we give our external team the parameters of the case we're working on, and they help us find the most appropriate products available. This helps us put together a solid plan for our clients and give them confidence in our opinion that these are the financial solutions that will serve them best in their unique situation.

CFP® DESIGNATION AND ONGOING TRAINING

This book is needed because there is so much misinformation on financial topics, and people are making major life decisions without having the proper facts and guidance. It's important to work with financial professionals who are highly trained. After years of college-level training and testing, I was proud to earn my Certified Financial Planner™ designation in 2003. In order to retain that designation, I'm required by the CFP® Board of Standards to complete a minimum of forty hours of continuing education every two years.

In addition to my continuing professional education, I voluntarily train with Ed Slott, a CPA in New York. Ed trains advisors like me who want to be a cut above everybody else in the Master Elite IRA Advisor Group.[4] To be part of it, I'm required to go to training sessions twice per year for three days at a time. There, I update my knowledge on taxes and retirement plans, including Roth IRAs, traditional IRAs, self-employed pension IRAs, 401(k)s, 403(b) s, 457 plans, and every other type of retirement plan. It's

---

4   Ed Slott's Elite IRA Advisor Group ("Ed Slott") is a membership organization. Qualifying criteria includes payment of annual dues and attendance of workshops. Membership with Ed Slott in no way implies that Jeffrey H. Massey is an IRA distribution expert. Ed Slott is not affiliated with Massey & Associates, Inc.

a significant expenditure of both time and money, but it's valuable and pertinent to my practice.

USE THIS BOOK AS YOUR GUIDE TO RETIREMENT

The goal of this book is to help you put together a financial roadmap, which is critical to having a successful retirement. After you've structured your financial roadmap, you'll be ready to confidently walk through that retirement door. Hopefully, you will sleep well at night knowing you've got your retirement income plan in place.

As we move forward into Chapter 1, we'll explore the wealth management formula I use for all of my clients. In Chapter 2, I'll go through the basics of Social Security and discuss the most important questions, such as: How do you make Social Security last? At what age should you begin taking your benefits?

In Chapter 3, I'll discuss strategies toward reducing your tax burden. This is what I affectionately call "disinheriting your Uncle Sam." In Chapter 4, you'll learn about the various types of investments and the risks you may be taking with your investment dollars. With a retirement plan, it is absolutely critical that you know what happens when your working days come to an end and have an income plan in place. I'll cover the importance of income planning and how to provide a Leveraged Legacy Plan™ for your family in Chapter 5.

Although I am not an attorney, I'll walk you through the importance of legal documents in Chapter 6. I'll discuss the structure of legal documents, and ask important questions such as:

- Who is in place to help you with your finances and financial decisions?
- Do you need a healthcare power of attorney?
- How do you transfer your assets to your family?

In Chapter 7, I'll encourage you to take a shot at retirement. You'll practice being retired and see if you can live on the dollars you expect to have in retirement. Lastly, in Chapter 8, I'll give you my suggestions for choosing a financial advisor who is right for you. I'll explain why I recommend working with a Certified Financial Planner™, and I'll give you the tools to help you pick the right advisor for yourself.

I have a passion for what I do. I've helped hundreds of people like you retire, and I want to continue to help hundreds more. As I often say on my radio show, you should choose an advisor who communicates with you on a level you're comfortable with. You don't want somebody who insults your intelligence or talks over your head using industry jargon that makes no sense to you. That won't help you feel comfortable or confident about your retirement plan.

It's important to trust the person you're working with, which is why I go deeper with each of my clients. I truly get to know each person, and I have an entire process built around doing that. We'll discuss your values, goals, and relationships. We'll talk about everything that's important to you in your life before we begin to talk about your assets and financial planning.

We'll also talk about your experiences with other advisors, including financial advisors, accountants, and attorneys. Then I'll talk a little bit more about my process, and how I take you through all the steps necessary to complete your plan. We'll discuss your deepest concerns. I'll ask what is truly important to you and learn what keeps you up at night. It's important for me to know those things so I can put together a plan that will hopefully make your fears fade away.

I'm grateful to work in a profession where I have the opportunity to help so many people. I wasn't able to help my parents retire or even improve their situation. They retired long before I became a financial planner. However, even after all of these years, part of me is still that scared little kid who is worried about finances. It drives me to work hard so I won't have to worry about my finances in the future.

Similarly, my goal is for you to be in a position where you will not need to worry about your financial future. By reading this book, my hope is to help you begin your own roadmap toward confidently and happily walking through the door of retirement.

As a fiduciary advisor, it's my responsibility to always do the right thing for my clients. And as my mother would tell you, it's also what I was raised to do.

Please grab a coffee and enjoy reading the rest of this valuable book. Let's continue along on this journey and see what we can accomplish together.

The Wealth Management Formula

Recently, a doctor heard me on the radio and came in to talk about his financial situation. Two or three minutes into the meeting, he abruptly said, "Look, I'm probably not like anybody you've ever met with before."

"Okay," I replied. "What does that mean?"

"Well," he said, "I don't know why anyone in their right mind would hire somebody to manage their money."

Obviously, being a financial advisor, I was a bit taken aback by that comment. I thought he was here to determine if I would be an advisor he would want to work with. "Fair enough," I said. "Why are you here?"

"Well, here's why," he said. "I can figure out what investments to go into and how to make my money grow. I've done pretty well." He had indeed done well growing his investments, and had more than $1 million set aside for his retirement. "What I don't know," he continued, "is how to take the money I have and turn it into a reliable stream of income."

The doctor's concern was a common one. Accumulating and growing money is a completely different skillset from creating a stream of income. Stockbrokers, for example, are focused on the accumulation and growth of dollars. They hope you never take money from your account because they want you to keep growing it. Retirement planning is very different and has a wider focus than accumulation.

ACCUMULATION VERSUS DECUMULATION

The doctor needed someone who specialized in income planning. Like many investors, he didn't know how to choose the appropriate products and investments for retirement, nor did he have access to the products without working with a financial advisor. In your retirement planning, you'll experience both an accumulation phase and a decumulation phase. Decumulation is the phase where you start taking your money for income and cash flow during retirement. After spending decades building up this money in the accumulation phase, it's now time to take the money and use it. What's the best way to go about doing that?

During retirement, most people do not have pensions but do have Social Security benefits. Some people are fortunate to have both pensions and Social Security benefits, and if so, they can generally retire with less money in savings.

The doctor was self-employed, so he didn't have any income from a company pension. He simply had the money he'd accumulated and grown. He did fine with building it up but had no idea how to turn it into a monthly paycheck in retirement to replace the paycheck he'd be giving up by closing his practice.

As an advisor who focuses on retirement planning, I help my clients generate a lasting and sustainable income during their retirement years. The average person will spend approximately twenty years in retirement, and some people are able to retire for thirty years or more. Therefore, it's critical to have an income plan that addresses both current cash flow and future growth. It's important to have a blend of places where you put your money. Often, certain types of insurance contracts are well suited for providing income, and stock market investments can be a good fit for growth potential.

There are different ways to generate a cash flow for my clients that will last throughout retirement. Some types of cash flows I create are guaranteed for the rest of an individual's life and are supported by the claims-paying ability of an insurance company. If every contract holder canceled and demanded their money, the company is legally required to have the reserves necessary to pay all investors. That can be a very reassuring level of protection for the people who utilize those products.

You don't get that same level of protection with variable-rate contracts, because variable contracts are invested directly in the stock market. It's critical for a piece of your retirement plan to provide a dependable income from a solid company. That becomes your baseline. If you have a guaranteed cash flow taking care of your necessities, then you can draw money from your growth bucket for all the fun stuff. If you need $10,000 to go on a big vacation, you just reach into your growth bucket and grab your money, because you don't need that money for your monthly cash flow.

WHEN CHANGE IS NECESSARY

The doctor was at a point where he wanted to retire, but did not know if he would have enough money to maintain his lifestyle. In my opinion, he did not yet have enough saved to replace his income and maintain his lifestyle.

His wife was also a doctor, and they felt they could add $50,000 per year to their retirement savings. This presented them with the option of continuing to work and building their retirement savings to reach a level that would support their lifestyle.

Adjusting your lifestyle is another option. This is not an easy step to take. It might require you to look at yourself in the mirror and say, "I know I've been spending five hundred dollars per month eating at restaurants, but do I really need to spend that? Are there other ways for me to have fun without spending quite so much money eating out?"

That can be a very tough conversation for people to have with themselves, and it is even tougher for me as a financial advisor. I often have to preface that conversation by saying, "Look, I would appreciate it if you don't shoot the messenger on this idea, but it might be time to consider adjusting your lifestyle to meet your retirement goals."

Sometimes we need to have that tough conversation. It's not mean or vicious. It's just tough because it's an uncomfortable conversation to have. As a fiduciary advisor, I am required to work in the best interest of the client, and that means being fully transparent and truthful. If there aren't enough dollars to continue supporting your current lifestyle, you'll either have to reduce your spending or continue working. Those are the hard facts. A third option is to work part time in retirement, which can have a dramatic and positive financial impact during your retirement years.

AVOIDING LOSS IS CRUCIAL

Again, my bias is to protect against financial downturns and avoid losses. This is important in both the accumulation phase and the decumulation phase. Many people evaluate investments by looking at the average annual rate of return, but that can be dangerous to the growth and preservation of your dollars.

Let's look at an example. From 2000 through 2015, the Vanguard S&P 500 Index averaged an annual rate of return of 5.67 percent. A different hypothetical investment portfolio averaged 5.66 percent, an almost identical average rate of return. When you look at those two average rates of return, what would you think? Would it really matter which account you had your money in?

Most people would look at that and think that 0.01 percent in the rate of return wouldn't make that much difference. Those people would be correct, if the funds performed identically each year. However, they didn't.

If you'd invested $1 million in the Vanguard S&P 500 Index Fund from 2000 to 2015, averaging 5.67 percent annually in returns, you would've ended that period with just over

$1,850,000. If you'd invested in the hypothetical portfolio with the slightly lower 5.66 percent average annual rate of return, you would've ended up with $2,350,000. You would have earned $500,000 *more*, with a *lower* average annual rate of return. How is that possible?

In one word: losses. An average annual rate of return does not tell you the complete story, when losses are involved. You need to dig much deeper to understand the impact of volatility and losses. It's not what you make that counts; it's what you don't lose when the stock market drops.

The Sharpe ratio helps us understand the efficiency of your portfolio. This ratio is a measure for calculating risk-adjusted return, and it's become the industry standard for such calculations. The Sharpe ratio helps to answer the question, "Am I being rewarded adequately for the level of risk I'm taking in my portfolio?"

In my opinion, an efficient portfolio should have a Sharpe ratio of 1.0 or higher. Do you know the Sharpe ratio for your portfolio?

HOW IDENTICAL RATES OF RETURN CAN HAVE DIFFERING RESULTS

Let's take a deeper look at why it's dangerous to evaluate

investments based on their average rates of return alone when building a strategy to avoid losses.

The following table illustrates how two hypothetical investments with identical average rates of return can perform very differently. The fund that avoids losses achieves a higher balance over the same period.

FUND 1: STOCK MARKET INDEX FUND

	INVESTMENT BALANCE	RATE OF RETURN
Start	$1,000,000	—
Year One	$1,113,200	11.32%
Year Two	$1,050,193	-5.66%
Year Three	$1,169,075	11.32%
Fund One Average Annual Rate of Return		5.66%

FUND 2: LESS VOLATILE ALTERNATIVE FUND

	INVESTMENT BALANCE	RATE OF RETURN
Start	$1,000,000	—
Year One	$1,056,600	5.66%
Year Two	$1,116,404	5.66%
Year Three	$1,179,592	5.66%
Fund Two Average Annual Rate of Return		5.66%

By avoiding losses, Fund 2 was able to earn $10,517 more than Fund 1. Avoiding loss leads to better growth and helps to preserve your assets. Warren Buffett, the wealthiest investor on the planet, says he has two rules:

- Rule number one: don't lose money.
- Rule number two: refer back to rule number one.

As you retire and begin your decumulation phase, I focus on turning your assets into a reliable cash flow. As a fiduciary advisor, I'll look at the products and money management available to us and choose the options that I feel are the best to help you pursue your retirement income goals. From there, I'll monitor the financial performance of your investments and change management teams when necessary.

In your retirement years, you want your excitement to come from your lifestyle, not from your investments. I want your investments to be dull and boring in contrast to the up-and-down feeling of a roller coaster. You may not have the most exciting growth when the market goes up, but you can be confident knowing you have a plan designed to help you avoid a large loss of money during market crashes.

When your friends are lamenting a stock market crash and all the money they lost, you'll be able to relax and realize you didn't take a big hit like your friends did. You'll realize how well I've structured your retirement plan to avoid major downturns. There's nothing sexy about that, but it's exactly what I want for my clients: solid financial planning and asset structuring that minimizes losses during market corrections.

THE WEALTH MANAGEMENT FORMULA

Spectrum Consultants is an international advisory firm for

financial advisors and CPAs, and I utilize their powerful wealth management formula. This definition of wealth management can be encapsulated by the formula WM = IC + AP + RM.

WM stands for wealth management, which is the sum total of the components we're defining here. Let's break down the remaining parts of the formula and learn how they contribute to the equation of wealth management.

PART ONE: INVESTMENT CONSULTING

Investment consulting (IC) is the first component of wealth management. Avoiding the loss of money is the number-one goal of the people we work with.

PART TWO: ADVANCED PLANNING

AP stands for advanced planning. Advanced planning is too complex to be described simply, so it has its own formula: AP = WE + WT + WP + CG. WE stands for wealth enhancement, WT is wealth transfer, WP is wealth protection, and CG is charitable giving.

Wealth Enhancement

Wealth enhancement accounts for cash flow in retirement. This includes a general income plan, Social Security strategies, and tax mitigation. We want to limit the tax hit during your lifetime, as well as after your lifetime in the transfer of assets to your family.

Wealth Transfer

Wealth transfer refers to the strategic and efficient transfer of your assets. To accomplish this, I often use what I call a "Leveraged Legacy Plan™." This is how we maximize the value of assets by converting highly taxed investments into an income-tax-free benefit for beneficiaries.

Wealth transfer would also include trust work, if necessary. In Rhode Island, under current rules for 2017, estate taxes need to be paid on the transfer of assets totaling more than $1,515,153. At the federal level, estate taxes are owed on the transfer of assets totaling more than $5,490,000 (for 2017). If you have an estate that large, congratulations! You're in the very small percentage of people who may end up paying some estate taxes, and trust work may be helpful toward minimizing your tax burden.

In addition to trusts, other legal documents can be utilized in managing wealth. Documents establishing the power of attorney can give people the ability to make specific decisions for you in the event you're unable to make those decisions yourself. The durable general power of attorney can be used to name a person, or more than one person acting together, to handle your financial affairs and decisions. A healthcare power of attorney document allows you to designate someone to make medical decisions to keep you well. This designated person will then be able to choose the doctors, treatments, or hospitals that are best for you.

Of course, you should meet with an attorney for all of your legal advice. These are very personal documents and decisions.

Lastly, what do you want to be done medically in your final stages of life? If you are noncommunicative, and you cannot blink or lift a finger, do you want to be kept alive artificially? Or would you rather have further treatment withheld? It's a tough decision that affects your family, and in my opinion, it's best for you to make this decision in advance instead of forcing your family members to make this very difficult decision.

I've personally been involved with three family deaths that involved a living will. For your family, losing you will be awful, and it will be difficult for them to decide whether to withhold treatment in your final days. Creating a living will allows you to make those important decisions now and not burden your children with the responsibility of making those decisions during the difficult time of your passing.

Wealth Protection

Wealth protection is the next part of the equation for the advanced planning component of wealth management. Wealth protection can include legal, accounting, and insurance considerations. Based on the type of business you're in, there might be an ideal legal structure for your assets, such as a limited liability company.

You might be advised to add an umbrella policy to your homeowner's insurance for personal or business liability. This is common for people who own rental property, because it's easy to be sued in that business. It's also common for people who work in high-risk, litigious environments like healthcare or commercial real estate. It's important to protect your assets.

Charitable Giving

The final piece of the advanced planning equation is charitable giving. Charitable giving is a goal of approximately one in three people I work with. This charitable giving can focus on their favorite nonprofit organization, alma mater, church, or even hospital. For example, I had a client who made a sizeable donation to a hospital after his wife passed away because he was thankful for their extensive efforts to keep her healthy and treat her cancer.

As part of wealth management, we help people achieve

their charitable giving goals in the most efficient way possible. For example, if you are age seventy and a half, you can give money directly from your IRA to a charity. Doing so will satisfy your required minimum distributions from the IRA under the current tax law.

PART THREE: RELATIONSHIP MANAGEMENT

In the third part of the wealth management formula, RM stands for relationship management. When necessary, relationships might need to be managed with partnering attorneys, accountants, or risk managers.

For example, two young clients of mine owned thirty-eight rental properties. When we first met, I learned that they had been paying for individual insurance policies on each property. I had a relationship with a risk manager, so I put them in touch. The risk manager helped to consolidate those policies, and he saved my clients a significant amount of money.

With another recent case, my client mentioned they were paying about $3,900 for their homeowner's insurance. That seemed high to me based on the property size, so I referred her to a property and casualty insurance advisor that I work closely with. Sure enough, they were paying too much! Their new annual premium is just over $2,000. That is a nearly 50 percent reduction in the cost of their homeowner's insurance. Needless to say, it proved beneficial for me to review their expenses with them.

We handle a wide range of services for our clients. By doing everything in the wealth management formula, we bring a massive amount of value to the table for our clients. Investment brokers, on the other hand, typically are not going to do much beyond the investment consulting. This is part of the advantage of hiring a true financial planner for your wealth management. A good financial planner will give you a comprehensive review of all of your estate issues.

WHAT HAPPENED WITH THE DOCTOR?

The doctor's experience ended well. He felt confident in the products and services I was able to bring to the table because I have access to products that individual investors don't have direct access to.

To access insurance-based products, you're required to have contracts with the insurance companies and a professional license to sell insurance. With investment products, individual investors often need a minimum of $1 million to access institutional money managers. However, through our relationship with AE Wealth Management, LLC, clients with smaller amounts to invest can access institutional money managers. By working with one of our professional financial planners, you can build a better team to work on your behalf.

Our focus is to help people who are nearing retirement. If you're within five to seven years of retirement, now is a great time to begin structuring your holdings in a manner that will maximize their value for you and your family when you're ready to retire.

MOST IMPORTANTLY: START NOW

The most common question I get is, "Do I have enough money to retire?" Unfortunately, many people do not have enough money to be in a solid position to retire. A large percentage of people have not saved adequately for their retirement and will have difficulty in their retirement years. Ultimately, they may become a burden on their families.

According to a fact sheet recently released by the Social Security Administration,[1] 39 percent of workers report that they have no savings set aside for retirement. Those people will likely rely on their Social Security payments for all their income during retirement, and that's not a rosy picture to paint.

---

1   "Fact Sheet," Social Security Administration, https://www.ssa.gov/news/press/factsheets/basicfact-alt.pdf.

If you don't have a plan in place, start one now. There's an old saying that the best time to plant a tree for shade was twenty years ago, and the second-best time is today. You just need to start, because the journey of a thousand miles begins with a single step. Start saving now, even if you can only save ten dollars per week. The earlier you start, the better off you will be when it's time to retire.

Social Security

While working with my clients, much of what I do involves Social Security benefits. There is so much about Social Security that most people do not understand. A few years ago, a husband and wife came in to meet with me and gave me a good overview of their situation. They told me they were very involved with their finances, and read financial magazines like *Kiplinger's* and *Money* every single month.

"Well that's wonderful," I told them, because they seemed well-informed. As we were reviewing their assets and income, I asked them about their Social Security retirement benefits. The husband told me his monthly benefit amount that he was receiving. His wife, however, did not expect to receive any Social Security benefits at all. "Oh no," she said. "I don't qualify. I never worked outside the home. I just raised my children and never really had an outside job."

I was stunned. They regularly read multiple financial magazines but somehow did not know that she was eligible to receive a spousal benefit due to her husband's work history and his eligibility for benefits. When I told them about the spousal benefit she could receive, they didn't believe it was truly possible, so I gave them a homework assignment: inquire about the spousal benefit with the Social Security administration, and we'll review the results at our next meeting.

When they came back in to see me, they had some great news: she qualified for the spousal retirement benefit and would now receive over one thousand dollars per month. They were seventy years old and had been leaving this money on the table for four years. He had been taking his Social Security benefit payments since he was sixty-six years old, but she had not applied for (or even known about) the spousal benefit she could have been receiving at the same time. They were very grateful to receive the extra income.

Even though many people feel well-informed about their finances, it's tough to beat a financial professional who does this for a living every day. This is especially true if you're able to work with a Certified Financial Planner™, as the CFP® designation is generally regarded as one of the most recognized and respected designations in the world of financial planning.

THE BACKGROUND OF SOCIAL SECURITY

Social Security was approved by President Roosevelt in 1935, and the first benefits were paid out in 1940. The first check was paid to a woman by the name of Ida May Fuller, who received a monthly benefit of $22.54. She began receiving her benefit at the age of sixty-five, and she lived to be one hundred years old.

Although she received payments for thirty-five years, she only worked for three years within the Social Security system. She earned wages totaling $2,475 and paid a total of twenty-four dollars and seventy-five cents into the Social Security system. Every month for thirty-five years, she received nearly her entire contribution back. She was paid $22,888.92 in Social Security benefits over her lifetime. It was rare for people in her generation to live to be one hundred years old, although many people today are achieving that feat. When Social Security was created in 1935, the average life expectancy was just sixty-two years of age, so Ida lived well beyond the average!

HOW IS SOCIAL SECURITY FUNDED?

Social Security is funded through a tax called the Federal Insurance Contribution Act (FICA), which began in January of 1937. Through 2009, the Social Security trust fund has collected $13.8 trillion and paid out $11.3

trillion.[1] Over 450 million Americans have been issued a Social Security number,[2] and at the time of this writing, over 66 million people are currently receiving benefits from this system.[3]

On the Social Security Administration's website, there's a chart illustrating the number of workers per retiree in America. The chart's data shows how this ratio has changed in the past and how it's projected to change in the future. If you'd like to see each year of past data since 1940, and the projected data for the future, the chart is currently located at www.ssa.gov/history/ratios.html.

The chart shows a steep decline in the number of workers paying into Social Security compared to the number of retirees who are receiving benefits. When Social Security began in 1940, there were 159 workers per retiree. Five years later, that number fell to forty-two workers per retiree, and the number continued to fall from there. As of 2017, there are 2.8 people working for every one retiree, and it's expected to be only 2.2 workers per retiree by 2035.

---

1   "Frequently Asked Questions," Social Security Administration, https://www.ssa.gov/history/hfaq.html.

2   Carolyn Puckett, "The Story of the Social Security Number," Social Security Administration, https://www.ssa.gov/policy/docs/ssb/v69n2/v69n2p55.html.

3   "Fast Facts & Figures About Social Security, 2017," Social Security Bulletin 69, no. 2, 2009, https://www.ssa.gov/policy/docs/chartbooks/fast_facts/2017/fast_facts17.html.

In 2017 there were over forty-eight million Americans who were at least sixty-five years old, and that number is projected to increase to seventy-nine million people by 2035. That's an increase of over *64 percent* in only eighteen years.

HOW SOCIAL SECURITY BENEFITS WORK

In Social Security terminology, PIA stands for primary insurance amount, which is the dollar amount of the retirement benefit you would qualify for if you started your benefits at your full retirement age (FRA). Your full retirement age is an age designated by Social Security, and it's determined by the year you were born. You'll also have the option to take a partial benefit at an earlier age for a reduced benefit. Let's take a look at the different retirement ages and benefits posted on the Social Security website (www.ssa.gov) as of 2017.

Full Retirement and Age 62 Benefit By Year Of Birth

Year of Birth [1]	Full (normal) Retirement Age	Months between age 62 and full retirement age [2]	At Age 62 [3]			
			A $1000 retirement benefit would be reduced to	The retirement benefit is reduced by [4]	A $500 spouse's benefit would be reduced to	The spouse's benefit is reduced by [5]
1937 or earlier	65	36	$800	20.00%	$375	25.00%
1938	65 and 2 months	38	$791	20.83%	$370	25.83%
1939	65 and 4 months	40	$783	21.67%	$366	26.67%
1940	65 and 6 months	42	$775	22.50%	$362	27.50%
1941	65 and 8 months	44	$766	23.33%	$358	28.33%
1942	65 and 10 months	46	$758	24.17%	$354	29.17%
1943-1954	66	48	$750	25.00%	$350	30.00%
1955	66 and 2 months	50	$741	25.83%	$345	30.83%
1956	66 and 4 months	52	$733	26.67%	$341	31.67%
1957	66 and 6 months	54	$725	27.50%	$337	32.50%
1958	66 and 8 months	56	$716	28.33%	$333	33.33%
1959	66 and 10 months	58	$708	29.17%	$329	34.17%
1960 and later	67	60	$700	30.00%	$325	35.00%

1. If you were born on January 1st, you should refer to the previous year.

2. If you were born on the 1st of the month, we figure your benefit (and your full retirement age) as if your birthday was in the previous month. If you were born on January 1st, we figure your benefit (and your full retirement age) as if your birthday was in December of the previous year.

3. You must be at least 62 for the entire month to receive benefits.

4. Percentages are approximate due to rounding.

5. The maximum benefit for the spouse is 50 percent of the benefit the worker would receive at full retirement age. The percent reduction for the spouse should be applied after the automatic 50 percent reduction. Percentages are approximate due to rounding.

Source: www.ssa.gov/planners/retire/agereduction.html

This table illustrates that the full retirement age is different for people based on their year of birth. If you were born between 1943 and 1954, your full retirement age is sixty-six years old. If you were born in 1960 or after, your full retirement age is sixty-seven. For those in between the years 1954 and 1960, you would add two months per year. If you were born in 1955, for example, your full retirement age is sixty-six years and two months old. If you were born a year later in 1956, your full retirement age is sixty-six years and four months.

It's important to be aware of the options and numbers shown in this table. If your full retirement age is sixty-six, you have the option to take a partial retirement benefit earlier at age sixty-two. If you do that, however, you'll be hit with a *25 percent* reduction in your retirement benefit. Similarly, if your full retirement age is sixty-seven years of age, and you take the early benefit option at age sixty-two, you will lose *30 percent* of the primary insurance amount you would have received at your full retirement age.

If you take the early benefit, that's your payment going forward. You won't be eligible to receive the larger benefit amount when you reach your full retirement age. There have been a number of times where a prospective client has come into my office and shown me their Social Security statement, believing they would receive the partial benefit at age sixty-two and then get bumped up to the full primary insurance amount at age sixty-seven. Unfortunately, that's not how it works. The only way your benefit amount increases is if social security declares a cost-of-living adjustment.

As of 2017, the cost-of-living adjustment is based on the Consumer Price Index for Urban Wage Earners and Clerical Workers (CPI-W). It is the wrong index to use, in my humble opinion. This index measures the rise in wages, not the rise in living costs. It's problematic for retirees because wages are completely disconnected from the cost of living of retirees. The annual increases in retirees' cost of living are driven by medical expenses, prescription drugs, food, gasoline, and many other rising expenses that are not tied to urban wages. It's very unfortunate for retirees that the index used for cost of living adjustments is not related to their actual cost of living.

SHOULD YOU TAKE YOUR BENEFITS EARLY?

For many people, it's better to wait until your full retirement age and receive your full primary insurance amount. Are there exceptions to this rule? The simple answer is yes. Of course there are exceptions. For example, you may want to draw your benefit early if you are experiencing bad health and are unsure whether you'll live to your full retirement age. There are other scenarios as well. In determining the ideal point in time to take your benefits, it becomes all about the math.

Let's assume that your full retirement age is sixty-six years old and your primary insurance amount is $1,000 per month. If you start at age sixty-two, your monthly benefit will be reduced by 25 percent to $750. If you choose not to take the early benefit and instead wait until age sixty-six to take your full benefit, you're leaving money on the table for those four years. The $750 monthly benefit would total $36,000 in the forty-eight months you could have received the early retirement benefit.

The full retirement benefit of one thousand dollars per month is $250 more than the early benefit. At what point would you come out ahead by waiting to take the full retirement benefit and foregoing the $36,000 of early payments? To answer that question, you divide $36,000 by the $250 additional monthly benefit, and you arrive at the answer of 144 months, which is exactly twelve years. The question then becomes, do you expect to live to age seventy-eight? If you think that might be rolling the dice a little too aggressively for you, then you may want to take your retirement benefit early at age sixty-two at the reduced amount. It is not uncommon for people to live well into their eighties and nineties as medical technology is keeping us healthier as we age.

ENHANCED BENEFITS AND OPTIONS

If you defer your payments past your full retirement age, you'll receive a slightly higher benefit amount for every month that you defer. Currently, that rate is 8 percent per year, and it's prorated on a monthly basis. You'll get an increase of one-twelfth of 8 percent for each month that you defer your payments beyond your full retirement age. If your full retirement age is sixty-six years old and you defer your payments until age seventy, you can get 8 percent more for each year, multiplied by four years for a total of 32 percent more money going into your pocket every month.

If you're married, deferring your benefits may be more appealing. By utilizing spousal benefits (if you qualify), you may have a shorter period of time to break even by taking a spousal benefit at your full retirement age while deferring your own benefit. Let's look at some hypothetical examples to illustrate my point.

If you qualified for a full retirement benefit of $1,000 per month at age sixty-six, you could wait until age seventy to take your payments and receive $320 more per month for a total of $1,320 dollars per month. In waiting until age seventy, you've left $48,000 on the table (four years of monthly payments of one thousand dollars). If you divide $48,000 by the extra $320 per month you'll get at age seventy, it gives you the answer that it would take 150 months (twelve and a half years) to break even.

There's a very good twist to this story, if you're married and eligible to draw from your spouse's benefit. Let's extend our earlier hypothetical example and say that your spouse also qualifies for the same benefit of $1,000 per month at the same full retirement age of sixty-six years old. In this case, you could potentially draw a spousal benefit of $500 per month based on her work record and eligibility. This is significant because it reduces the amount of money you're leaving on the table, and it reduces the number of years until you would break even and benefit from deferring your full benefit payments.

Instead of leaving $48,000 on the table, you're now only foregoing $24,000 because you're receiving the $500 spousal payment each month for four years. If you divide this new number of $24,000 by the extra $320 you'll receive each month at age seventy, it now only takes seventy-five months (six and a quarter years) for you to break even, compared to the twelve and a half years it would've taken to break even without the spousal benefit. This is an example of how married people have an absolute advantage, and as an advisor, I calculate the benefits to determine what I refer to as the "sweet spot" to determine the best age for my clients to begin taking their Social Security retirement benefits.

ADDITIONAL BENEFITS FOR SURVIVORS AND DIVORCEES

Survivor benefits are also a common reason people defer their full retirement benefits and hold out for a larger benefit amount. When a married person passes away and a surviving spouse remains, the survivor keeps the higher of the two individual Social Security benefits.

For example, if the husband had a monthly benefit amount of $3,000 and the wife had a benefit of $1,800, the wife would receive a new benefit of $3,000 if her husband were to pass away before she did. Technically, she keeps her benefit of $1,800 and then receives $1,200 of her husband's former benefit, but it's simpler to remember that the survivor will get the higher value of the two.

Many people have the misconception that the surviving spouse will receive the full amount of their spouse's benefits upon their death, in addition to their own benefit, but that's not the case. It's an unfortunate misunderstanding that I find often when educating people about what they can and can't expect to receive from Social Security.

If you're now divorced and you were married for at least ten years, you may qualify to draw a spousal benefit from your ex-spouse's earnings record, assuming that you have not remarried. This can be an important benefit for many people whose spouse's earning record is much greater than their own.

Under current regulations, if you are at full retirement age and were sixty-two years old before January 1, 2016, you could file a restricted application on the spousal benefit to draw 50 percent of your ex-spouse's retirement benefit while letting your own retirement benefit defer (and increase) until age seventy. You would then go back to Social Security and refile for your own benefit when you turned seventy years old.

Social Security is a very complex topic, and the rules will likely change in the future. Therefore, it's important to work with a financial planner who stays up to date on current and upcoming changes affecting your Social Security benefits. As a professional working in the retirement niche, it's important for me to stay on top of these changes. To remain informed on the present and future details of not just Social Security but retirement planning in general, I attend an average of ten conferences per year. If you're selecting an advisor, you might want to ask, "How many conferences have you been to in the last year?" If they say, "One or two," are they really staying updated on the industry?

HOW CAN SOCIAL SECURITY BE SUSTAINED?

Sustaining Social Security in its current form will be an

ongoing challenge. One simple solution has been proposed by a very intelligent Certified Financial Planner™ by the name of Michael Kitces. He's a highly technical guy and has more letters behind his name than any person I've ever met. At a conference I attended, he once explained that our government could satisfy all Social Security needs for the next one hundred years if individual workers and employers each paid an additional 1.35 percent in FICA tax.

In my opinion, adding 1.35 percent in taxes to keep Social Security funded for one hundred more years is a simple and relatively painless solution. What bothers me is that this type of technical analysis is out there, but politicians don't seem to want to pay attention to it. When they look at "fixing" Social Security, they focus on things like changing your benefit amount or changing when you can apply for benefits. Why don't we just fix the funding formula so the program can take care of itself? If you asked a group of twenty-year-old workers whether it would be worth 1.35 percent in additional taxation to ensure Social Security would be there for them in forty-five years, I would be surprised if anyone answered no to that question.

The federal deficit is also out of control, which makes it even more difficult for the government to support the benefits of Social Security. It has been widely reported that to sustain Social Security, they'll have to change the funding formula, or retirees will need to take a reduced benefit, or both.

Additionally, with the federal deficit, income taxes will likely need to go up at some point. Currently, retirees pay taxes on a maximum of 85 percent of their Social Security income. Using what's called the provisional income formula, the Internal Revenue Service determines how much of your retirement benefit is taxable, and the current range is 0 to 85 percent. People with the lowest incomes may not have any of their Social Security benefit taxed, but people with the highest incomes may be taxed on as much as 85 percent of their benefit. However, at any point, the government could decide to tax everybody on 100 percent of their Social Security, and the federal deficit could be part of the reason the government may make that decision. I am not convinced that the politicians would do this because retirees vote and the politicians don't want to lose their next election.

In determining how much of your Social Security benefits will be taxable, the provisional income calculation currently includes all streams of income (even tax-free forms of income, like municipal bonds) along with 50 percent of your Social Security benefit. If your total income is between $25,000 and $34,000 (or $32,000 and $44,000 for married couples), you will pay taxes on up to 50 percent of your Social Security benefit. If your income is higher than $34,000 for singles (or $44,000 for married couples), you'll be taxed on up to 85 percent of your Social Security benefit. If the entirety of your income comes from your Social Security benefit, under the current tax structure, you will not likely be taxed on your Social Security benefit.

Currently, if you're married but file your taxes separately, you are automatically taxed on up to 85 percent of your Social Security. There is no provisional income calculation for this scenario currently. They simply apply the tax and take any tax breaks away from you. This is one of the many reasons to work with a Certified Public Accountant who understands Social Security and compares all options to find your best outcome from the standpoint of taxation. Our goal is to help people save tax dollars and pay the IRS the least amount allowed by law.

SUMMARY

Social Security is just one part of your retirement plan, but it is a very important piece of the puzzle. It's crucial to know your sweet spot when it comes to Social Security planning and to understand the best approach for your financial situation.

Similar to the client of mine who bought his dream car, you may benefit greatly by working with an experienced retirement planner. Social Security employees are not allowed to discuss investment strategies or retirement planning strategies with you. They can answer any questions you have about Social Security, but they're not permitted to advise you on your best financial strategy.

Therefore, you want to work with a "retirement tour guide" to coordinate your different sources of income, maximize your Social Security retirement benefit, and minimize your taxation. My goal is to help my clients receive the most money possible on a monthly basis for the remainder of their lives so they can fulfill their dreams of a comfortable and enjoyable retirement.

Disinherit Your Uncle

In early 2016 the Northern Rhode Island Chamber of Commerce held a breakfast meeting for local business owners. The guest speaker was from the United States Chamber of Commerce in Washington, DC, and he spoke about the future of taxation. More specifically, he spoke about income taxes and their relation to our enormous (and growing) federal deficit and expenses.

He showed us a slide to illustrate his point, and he called it his "Pac-Man Slide" because it resembled the famous video game character. The illustration looked like three separate Pac-Man characters. The first Pac-Man had its mouth open the widest, the second was less open, and the third was barely open at all. The first two characters represented our actual government expenditures in 2000 and 2015, and the final character illustrated the projected expenditures in 2026.

In 2000, fifty-eight cents of every dollar collected in federal taxes was used to fund Social Security, Medicare, and Medicaid, and pay interest on the national debt. In 2015, that number had grown to seventy-eight cents per dollar collected. The growth didn't stop there, however. The third and final Pac-Man of the slide illustrated the government's projected expenses in 2026: a staggering *ninety-six cents of every dollar collected* will be needed for Social Security, Medicare, Medicaid, and debt payments. That should scare all of us, and it should get our attention regarding the high likelihood that income taxes will be going up in the not-too-distant future.

David Walker formerly served the United States as its general comptroller, which is a position I affectionately call the "head bean counter." A comptroller is the person who keeps their eye on the debt level of an organization—the entire United States in this case. Walker went on to become CEO of the Peter G. Peterson Foundation, which (according to their website) has a mission to "increase public awareness of the nature and urgency of the key fiscal challenges threatening America's future and to accelerate action on them."

In a 2009 article posted on CNN.com, Walker delivered an eye-opening warning about the future of taxation in America. "Unless we begin to get our fiscal house in order," he wrote, "there's simply no other way to handle our ever-mounting debt burdens except by doubling taxes over time. Otherwise, our growing commitments for Medicare and Social Security benefits will gradually squeeze out spending on other vital programs such as education, research and development, and infrastructure."[1]

Let's think about that. If you're currently retired and in a 25 percent tax bracket, this means that you may soon be paying a tax rate of 50 percent. Even if he's only half-correct in his predictions, it's possible you'll still be paying 37 percent of your income to the government in taxes. The problem for retirees is that most of them have their wealth in qualified retirement plans that will be taxed upon distribution. These retirees will be severely impacted if tax rates rise as significantly as Walker predicts.

Tax-qualified plans were born in the 1970s, when the highest income tax bracket was 70 percent. The intent was that you'd be able to save money pretax, avoid the highest taxation levels, and pay taxes on your investments in retirement at a tax rate expected to be much lower. This made sense at a time in history when you could be taxed at a rate of 70 percent. In 2017, however, the highest tax rate is 39.6 percent, and most people pay between 15 and 25 percent of their income in taxes.

1   David W. Walker, "Commentary: Why your taxes could double," CNN Politics, April 15, 2009, http://www.cnn.com/2009/POLITICS/04/15/walker.tax.debt/index.html.

Are today's tax rates the lowest you will ever see or the highest you'll ever see? If you ask a twenty-year-old this question, you'll commonly find that they expect to pay more taxes when they are older. Regardless of age, if you know anything about finances, the federal government, and the federal deficit level, then you know that it is likely we will pay more income taxes in the future.

STRATEGIES TO PROTECT AGAINST RISING TAXES

Due to the possibility of a future with higher income taxes, one strategy is to put your money away after you have paid taxes on it. This is an especially good idea for younger investors, and one of the most popular vehicles to use for this purpose is the Roth IRA. A Roth IRA is funded by money you've already been taxed on (after-tax contributions), and it grows in a tax-deferred manner, meaning there are no taxes on investment gains as the account is growing. Additionally, assuming you play by the rules, your money and investment gains are not taxed when they are paid out to you, resulting in an income that will be free of income taxes for the rest of your life, based on current tax rules. The two rules that you must comply with to gain this great tax-free benefit are simple: the Roth IRA must have been established for at least five years, and you must have reached age fifty-nine and one half.

If you're currently retired, a Roth IRA can still be strategically valuable in legacy planning as a vehicle to efficiently transfer wealth to your heirs. For example, if you have a big chunk of money in a 401(k) and you know you will not need that money during your lifetime, you may be able to shift those dollars into a Roth IRA. You will pay income taxes on that money now, upon converting the structure to a Roth IRA, but it can be beneficial to your heirs. Currently, you can pass on a Roth IRA to your spouse, and then again to your children and/or grandchildren. The investments continue to grow in a tax-free manner, and the income can be tax-free for the rest of their lives, as well. It is a cool strategy many people ignore but probably shouldn't. It can be a fabulous way to pass money to your heirs on a tax-free basis.

If you're fortunate enough to have a retirement plan at work that offers a Roth structure—a 401(k) Roth, for instance—then by all means, take advantage of that. Under current law, you can contribute higher amounts at older ages. You can contribute $18,000 into those plans regardless of your age, but if you're age fifty or above, you can contribute a total of $24,000 annually (in 2017).

In Traditional and Roth IRAs, you can currently contribute an additional $1,000 per year if you're fifty years old or older (contributing a maximum of $6,500 annually, as opposed to $5,500 for everyone else). There are income qualifications and limitations for IRA contributions, and tax laws may change after the time of this writing, so you'll want to utilize a qualified accountant or financial advisor for up-to-date information if these strategies are of interest to you.

ADDITIONAL TAX-ADVANTAGED OPTIONS

As I've mentioned, there are contribution limits to both Roth IRAs and 401(k) Roth plans. However, the insurance industry has another option for you in which there are no limits to the amount of money you contribute each year. If you're a business owner and you, first and foremost, need death-benefit protection for your beneficiaries, this can also be a way to use after-tax money to help you build assets on a tax-deferred basis. The insurance product used for this is generally referred to as a "cash value life insurance contract," and there are many different types. The type I tend to prefer for many of my clients is called an "indexed universal life insurance contract." There are many different types of life insurance policies out there, so it's important to have your advisor do the shopping for you and compare the various products to determine the one that is the best fit for your circumstances.

These life insurance policies are structured very differently from traditional life insurance. Most people view life insurance as a bill and want to spend the least amount of money each month and receive the highest possible benefit from it upon death. That's why temporary (term) life insurance is so popular. You pay a small amount for a high amount of coverage, but the downside is that term insurance becomes more expensive in your later years, and you don't build any cash value with the premiums that you pay.

The indexed universal life insurance contracts we like to work with are positioned and utilized in a way that is similar to corporation-owned life insurance. Corporations understand they can plow money into these policies and have it grow on a tax-deferred basis, while also having access to their money via loans. While providing the desired amount of death benefits, it's also often used as a tool to build up cash value.

There are IRS regulations requiring a corridor between the cash value and the death benefit. If the cash value gets too close to the death benefit, the IRS could declare that it should be considered an investment instead of an insurance product. If it's an investment, it could become fully taxable and lose its tax advantages. These policies are typically structured to account for those rules. As the cash value builds up within the policy, if it gets too close to the amount of the death benefit, the company increases the death benefit to comply with IRS rules. If the cash value is too close to the death benefit, the IRS could disqualify the death benefit as income-tax-free and tax all the growth within the policy. Obviously, that would not be a good outcome! By pushing up the death benefit, the cash value can continue to grow higher.

Tax-deferred growth is the primary reason I like the structure of indexed universal life insurance contracts. In many cases, you have the potential for double-digit rates of growth (assuming the market goes up by double digits) with favorable tax treatment. Additionally, these types of contracts offer protection against losses. Interest earnings are linked to the performance of an external market index, such as the S&P 500 Index, but your money is never actually invested in the market. As of the writing of this book, it's possible to have an indexed universal life insurance contract with a 10 percent cap on annual earnings. In that case, if the S&P 500 Index goes up 12 percent, you hit the cap, and 10 percent interest is credited into your insurance contract. If the S&P 500 Index gains 7 percent the next year, you get all of the 7 percent because it's within the 10 percent cap.

Here is the critically important benefit available within these contracts: your interest earnings are locked in annually. If the market goes down by 20 percent, you earn zero for that year, but you keep all the dollars you've gained in previous years.

Think about that. If you never experience a loss, and you

receive interest credits tied to the gains of the market, do you think you would be doing well over the course of many years? The math proves that answer to be yes. During the decade spanning from 2000 to 2009—the worst decade in the history of the stock market—the S&P 500 Index lost an average of 1 percent per year. Many people lost a significant amount of their retirement savings. During that worst decade, using the above referenced hypothetical indexed universal life insurance contract, you would have averaged about a 5 percent *gain* per year by locking in the gains in the up years and avoiding the losses in the down years. That is the power of not losing money while still having the opportunity to participate and share in the upside of market gains.

Indexed universal life insurance is not a direct investment in the stock market. It is an insurance product that provides death benefit protection, first and foremost, with guarantees backed by the financial strength and claims-paying ability of the issuing company. It provides the potential for interest to be credited based in part on the performance of specific indexes without the risk of loss of premium due to market downturns or fluctuation. It may not be appropriate for everyone.

Utilizing life-insurance products can fulfill two needs. First, we often call it a "self-completing plan" because it accomplishes its goal regardless of how long you live. If you need life insurance to protect your family or business, and you want to have access to the assets you've built toward retirement, it works well. If you live to be one hundred years old, you'll be able to enjoy the income benefits of the insurance product. If you pass away early, however, the death benefit feature of life insurance will complete your financial plan for your family. In that scenario, it is a self-completing plan that operates much differently than an IRA or 401(k), where you just get the actual cash balance upon your death.

While I've given a general overview of how insurance products can be used as part of your financial plan, there is a tremendous amount of detail with these types of contracts, and it is very important for you to receive an illustration from your advisor. Your advisor can show you the historical performance of each insurance product, as well as explain how they might perform in the future.

The National Association of Insurance Commissioners (NAIC) limits the percentage rate that can be used in illustrating potential future gains to assure that advisors' projections are realistic and sustainable. I completely agree with that approach.

When working with my clients and projecting the future growth of their insurance products, I actually use a *lower* rate than the maximum permitted rate. I would rather be more conservative—underpromise and overdeliver—than the other way around. In addition to showing the NAIC-approved rate, I also illustrate the outcome as if the worst decade in the history of the stock market repeated itself throughout the illustration period. In my opinion, that is being *very* conservative!

DISINHERIT YOUR UNCLE

By structuring your investments in a tax-efficient manner, you're effectively disinheriting your Uncle Sam in the present and the future. With many people agreeing that income taxes will likely be much higher in the future, it makes sense to pay taxes at today's lower rates. This disinherits your Uncle Sam for the future, and he won't be able to dig into your pocket when you receive tax-free income from Roth IRAs, 401(k) Roth plans, or life-insurance products via the loan provision.

As the gentleman from the US Chamber of Commerce showed us on his "Pac-Man slide," there's a full expectation that the increasing federal expenses and deficit will present a huge financial problem for the government in the not-so-distant future. As we get deeper into debt, we increase the likelihood of higher income taxes in the future. If taxes do indeed rise significantly, you'd be better off paying today's lower tax rate on your investments and avoiding the higher taxes of the future.

Tax mitigation is always a key part of my retirement planning process with clients. If there's a way to reduce your tax burden, I absolutely want to show you that. Recently, I met with a couple of prospective clients who were receiving money from a variable annuity. They had an income rider guaranteeing an income of $10,672 per year.

Their previous financial advisor told them they should begin taking those payments now, despite the fact they were still both working and earning six figures of income. I understand what the advisor meant, because the annuity had hit a limit and the couple should take those payments, or they'd simply be leaving that money on the table. If they didn't take those annuity payments, they wouldn't get any additional money or advantage in the future.

However, this advisor was more of a product broker who was essentially selling variable annuities. He was not really a financial planner, tax planner, or comprehensive financial advisor. If he had been, he likely would've advised a better option for this couple: transfer that annuity money directly into another IRA and defer the taxes until they really needed the income. That would've saved this couple thousands of dollars in taxes.

I also double-check assumptions in clients' eligibility to contribute to tax-advantaged plans. For example, this same couple had used H&R Block to file their income taxes. On her W-2 form, an important box was incorrectly checked off. It was the determination of whether she had a retirement plan at her employer. She did not, but the W-2 form indicated otherwise. The H&R Block representative missed it and didn't know enough about the client to realize the W-2 form had a critically important error.

As a result, the clients were told they could contribute a maximum of $2,700 into their IRA plans for that year. However, once the W-2 information was corrected, they were each able to maximize their IRA contributions and get favorable tax treatment on up to $13,000 that year. That means they were able to defer taxes on another $10,300 in that tax year. Assuming a federal tax rate of 25 percent and another 5 percent for state taxes, with a total taxable income reduction of $20,972, that would be a tax savings of over $6,000 for just that year!

That's the type of comprehensive financial planning I do for my clients, week in and week out. I look for every possible way to put more money in my clients' pockets, especially strategies that disinherit your Uncle Sam.

Investments and Risks

As an advisor, it's important to explain investments and financial issues in a manner that is easy to understand. When radio listeners call in to my weekly radio show *Massey on Money*™, they often tell me they appreciate the simple manner in which I explain financial information. I work hard to simplify complex financial strategies to help my listeners and clients better understand what we do and why it is beneficial to them.

One couple I work with has especially benefitted from this approach. The husband initially came into my office alone. "My wife definitely doesn't come to these meetings because she doesn't care about the finances," he said. I kindly asked if he would humor me and bring his wife along to the next meeting, and he did.

After the next meeting, as I sensed everything was going well and she was fully engaged in the process, I turned to her and asked, "I thought you didn't like these financial meetings?"

"Well," she said, "the other advisors we've worked with just talked over my head. I didn't understand anything they were talking about, but with you, I can finally understand what's going on with our money and what you're trying to accomplish for us."

I get those types of responses on a consistent basis, especially from the people who have listened to my radio show for months or years. People who are planning their retirement want to understand their financial situation and the advice being given to them, and it's gratifying to me to hear the feedback that I've conveyed valuable information in an understandable manner.

Many advisors are overly complicated in their communications because they're not focused on the outcome and benefits to the client. Investments could be compared to automobiles. There are different types of cars out there, but they effectively do the same thing: get you from point A to point B. When people shop for cars, most of them don't care about the complex technical details regarding the engine and how it operates. Instead, they're wondering what the outcome will be. What will this car do for me? How will it benefit me and meet my needs?

As an advisor, my job is to see your end goal and determine the best financial vehicle (or combination of vehicles) to get you where you want to go. It rarely makes sense to invest all your money in one area. There are pros and cons to each investment vehicle, whether it's stocks, bonds, insurance products, or other types of investments.

HOW TO EVALUATE INVESTMENT OPTIONS

When evaluating your investment options, it helps to make it as simple as possible. With that in mind, there are three features I would recommend using when choosing where to invest your money: safety, liquidity, and growth potential. Typically, you'll only get to choose two of those three features because safety and growth tend to be quite different.

For example, if you put your money in a savings account with your local bank, you will have liquidity because you can have access to your money very quickly. You'll have safety, as you will have the safety net of the FDIC coverage. However, with the current interest rates in place at most banks today, you can't expect to have any appreciable growth with bank accounts. At the current interest rates, you will not be keeping up with inflation.

I met with a client recently and was looking over their bank statements from a major bank. They had over $50,000 in a savings account that was labeled as "growth savings" on their statements. The interest rate was 0.01 percent. How can a financial institution have the audacity to call that a "growth savings" account?

Thankfully for people who wish to utilize savings accounts, market interest rates appear to be rising. The Federal Reserve raised rates in December of 2016 and again in March and June of 2017. It's projected that interest rates may be increased by one quarter of 1 percent one more time during 2017 and as many as three times in 2018. Only time will tell whether that happens, but a rising interest rate is important to keep in mind when looking at investment options, especially with bonds, as rising interest rates have a direct impact on the fair market value of bonds if you have to sell a bond prior to maturity. Also, rising interest rates can impact dividend-paying stock values as well.

Stock market investments are at the opposite end of the spectrum of safety. If you pick stocks, you have a much higher potential for growth, and you still have liquidity because you can sell your stock. However, you sacrifice safety, compared to a bank savings account.

Insurance products fall in the middle of the spectrum, in a variety of ways. Fixed annuities, for example, will be safer than stocks and typically have more growth potential than a bank savings account. You'll have less liquidity, however, when compared to savings accounts and shares of stock. Many annuities limit your access to a percentage of your principal. I have seen products that allow penalty-free withdrawals of 5 percent and 7 percent; however, most products allow penalty-free withdrawals of up to 10 percent of your money annually. You don't need me to tell you that if you withdraw that much each year, you will run out of money quickly! Even though that high withdrawal percentage is allowed, it is definitely not recommended.

When working with clients, we determine the ideal combination of investments that will offer them their desired levels of safety, liquidity, and growth potential. In each client's portfolio mix, we might need to choose some investments that offer safety and liquidity, as well as others offering growth potential. If the growth piece is a stock market investment, and the stock market goes down, the safer and more liquid investments can provide a safety net for the overall performance of your portfolio. Our clients tell us that this type of planning provides them peace of mind when it comes to an overall investment plan.

The specific allocation of investments is very subjective and varies from person to person. Some people do not have a high tolerance for risking the loss of their money, and may still be nervous having their money in a bank savings account. Others have a more aggressive approach toward their investments and want more growth to provide an enhanced income in retirement. Others fall somewhere in between, wanting the opportunity for moderate growth with protection against severe losses.

I work primarily with people who are retired or nearing retirement, and age is a huge factor when it comes to what they do with their money. The Certified Financial Planner™ board teaches an age-based standard for portfolio risk by using what's referred to as the rule of one hundred. Here's how it works: take the number one hundred, subtract your age, and that leaves you with the maximum percentage of your portfolio that should be in higher-risk investments. Using this standard, you should have no more than 40 percent of your investment portfolio at risk if you're sixty years old.

As we get closer to or further into retirement, it's normally best to transition to more conservative holdings with less risk of loss. This doesn't mean you cannot have any money in the stock market. It simply means you will want to have less volatile stocks in your portfolio investing in companies that are less likely to take a big hit if there's a market correction.

KEEPING INCOME NEEDS IN MIND

Your investment decisions should also factor in the income

needed in retirement. If you're putting all your money into a bank savings account at 0.01 percent interest, your money is safe, but I call this scenario "going broke safely." Inflation is currently running over 2 percent per year, so you'll actually be losing your money's purchasing power and going backward.

While bank savings accounts may not be ideal for growth against inflation, there is value to having a certain amount of money readily accessible. One of the biggest obstacles I see with people's portfolios is a lack of available, liquid money. It's not a bad thing to have a good chunk of money in the bank, whether it's $25,000 or even as much as $100,000. I call this "pillow money" because when your head hits the pillow at night, you are able to fall asleep knowing you have money in the bank that is easily accessible. This provides the peace of mind that many people want and need as they move forward in retirement. The downside here is that you will be losing purchasing power, as your money will not be growing enough, after taxes, to keep up with inflation.

INVESTING IN THE STOCK MARKET

When it comes to stock market investments, I often hear people say that if 100 percent of your money is in the stock market, you're taking too much risk. Generally, I would agree with that sentiment; however, there are different levels and types of risks, and diversifying your investments helps mitigate some risks.

There are many time-tested, established companies with decades of solid, consistent performance. Those types of companies tend to have much less risk than new and unproven companies, such as a high-tech company that is about to have their initial public offering. You could roll the dice with the new and unproven tech company, but you're taking a huge risk. It's possible to lose all of your money. Those are two simple examples of stock market investments with two different levels of risk.

Everyone's situation differs, but in general, I suggest that my clients should have a portion of their money allocated toward growth investment options like stocks. This offsets the safer investments in the portfolio, which come with the risk of losing purchasing power. However, it's important to avoid excessive exposure to risk, in the event of another massive stock market meltdown.

Many people recall and focus on the stock market crash of 2008, when the S&P 500 lost 37 percent of its value. However, if you look back to October of 2007 and track the S&P 500 through the bottom of the market decline in March of 2009, you would see that the S&P 500 Index actually lost *two-thirds* of its value! Think about that for a moment: *two-thirds* of its value in only eighteen months! If 100 percent of your money was invested there, you could've lost two-thirds of your retirement-income-producing assets. For most people, there would be no way they could retire with only one-third of the money they'd set aside for their retirement. After the market crash of 2008, I met with many people who had to postpone their retirements because of their overaggressive investment choices.

DON'T CHASE SHINY OBJECTS

When investing in the stock market, you should invest with prudence and make every attempt to remove your emotions from your decisions. It is fairly common to have pullbacks (5 percent reductions) and corrections (10 percent reductions) in the stock market. By the way, a 20 percent drop is defined as a "bear market." Although we haven't had a recession in years, that also happens in the stock market. It's not a question of if we will have another recession, it's when!

Mitigating the next recession is part of why the Fed is driven to raise the interest rates. If the interest rate can reach its target of 2 percent or more, it can be lowered again to stimulate the economy when the next recession comes. The interest rate is the Fed's primary tool to stimulate the economy. There's no guarantee this will fully prevent or reverse stock market losses, however, and that's why you should avoid chasing the next hot stock.

Remain focused on the larger picture instead of chasing shiny objects in the short term.

Stockbrokers may call you and say, "I've got an incredible deal for you. This company is going to skyrocket. You should sell your holdings in ABC company and buy XYZ company. The XYZ stock is going to take off, and you're going to be a millionaire from this deal." That's the kind of silliness that's out there in the investment world, and unfortunately, far too many people are mesmerized by these shiny objects and the illusion of fast, exponential returns.

When money is swindled away or outright stolen from investors, it's normally done by promising outrageous, above-market returns. A recent case in Rhode Island involved an advisor who allegedly told his clients they would earn an annual return of 30 percent on their money. It's absurd to believe that type of return would be possible in today's world, and yet he was able to lure in multimillionaires who wrote him checks for millions of dollars. The infamous example of Bernie Madoff in New York was a similar scenario with a similar result. Billions of dollars were swindled. These people were promised big returns, and anytime you invest in something expected to generate a large return, you have to assume that you could also experience a very large loss in value. The advisor stealing the money was not a risk that these investors considered.

One way to protect yourself against this type of risk is to invest in products and services that include third-party reporting. At Massey & Associates, Inc., we work with AE Wealth Management, LLC. They are an SEC Registered Investment Advisor firm. Fidelity is the custodian of our clients' investments, not my firm or AE Wealth Management, LLC. Fidelity provides the third-party involvement that gives our clients another layer of comfort.

With our retirement planning services, we are long-term planners. We don't attempt to time the market, and we don't focus on generating fast, short-term gains. If you have a short-term need and need your money back within a year or two, the stock market may not be the best place for you to be. Back in 2008, the popular television commentator Jim Kramer once said, matter-of-factly, that if you need your money back within five years, you shouldn't be in the stock market. The television executives called him on the carpet for that, and he spent the next week trying to spin what he'd said on all types of talk shows, but I believe his initial statement was accurate. If you need your money within the next five years, putting it in the stock market may not be the best idea. No one knows when the next big downturn will happen, nor does anyone know how long it will last.

What if the crash of 2008 happens again, when you're depending on that money to be there for you in three or four years? You're in trouble, because it will likely take much longer than that to regain your losses if history repeats itself. Bottom line: it's important to diversify in a way that matches your timeline and risk tolerance.

Removing emotion from your decisions also prevents the problem of selling low and buying high. It's common to see investors buy at a high point after a stock has made a significant gain, then sell at the low point after they've experienced losses. Those are often decisions driven by emotions instead of planning. It's a huge problem when investors have no plan or discipline in buying and selling.

In the 1990s, people seemed to enjoy telling me about their latest stock purchase. I would ask them what the price per share was when they bought it. Without exception, everyone knew that answer. That was their favorite part of the story, talking about how much they'd gained since they purchased the stock. My next question, however, always revealed the problem. "At what point do you intend to sell this stock?" I would ask.

I never heard an answer that reflected a disciplined strategy. Nobody ever replied, "Twelve dollars per share. If I bought it at ten dollars per share, and it goes up 20 percent to twelve dollars, I'll sell at that point and take my profits." Not one person said anything near that. Similarly, nobody had a plan in place to sell after a certain point of losses, which is equally important.

After the stock market crash, most of my social interaction around stock purchases came to an end. Nobody was talking about stocks anymore, because they were getting beat up and didn't have a plan. They got caught watching their shiny objects.

Another difficulty in the modern era is that the average person does not have the expertise to compete with the large institutions utilizing computerized algorithms. This new wave of computerized algorithms can buy and sell a stock in a nanosecond. When I first heard that term, I didn't even know what a nanosecond was. It's one-*billionth* of a second. Professional traders and their algorithms can identify a buying opportunity, buy the stock, and sell it within one-billionth of a second.

How are you going to compete with that, sitting at home on your computer? By the time you have access to the information, they're already in and out and done with the trade. This is one of the reasons I feel it's important to stay away from that type of short-term trading mentality and focus instead on your long-range strategy.

STOCK INVESTMENTS

Stock market returns are very different, depending on the time frame being measured. Stock market returns were actually negative from 2000 to 2009. Remember when the media dubbed it the lost decade? That's obviously not good, but generally you'll look at longer periods of time when assessing historical returns.

Our fundamental approach and bias is to mitigate the downside volatility. Typically, our clients will have a portion of their portfolio in stock market type investments. In addition to these market investments, we often allocate a portion of the portfolio for what we call a "protected position." These are most often fixed insurance contracts that are guaranteed by the claims-paying ability of the insurance carrier. The fixed insurance companies are required by law to have one dollar in reserve for every dollar of liability owed to investors. These required reserves provide a huge element of safety to the contract owner in the "safety position."

A simple example of a portfolio with a protected position is one that has a fifty-fifty split between market investments and protected positions. This allows you to participate in the growth potential of the stock and bond markets but remain protected by the lower-risk, fixed insurance products. For example, if the stock market goes down 10 percent, you may be down 10 percent but only on half of your money. In your protected position, you would have no losses at all, nor would you have made any money. Therefore, if you blend together those two rates of return, your portfolio will have lost only 5 percent in that economic downturn. It's a very simple way to mitigate the risk of heavy losses within your investment plan. Please keep in mind that this is only an example. A fifty-fifty split isn't for everybody, and we rarely split assets like that. I recommend that you meet with your advisor to determine the best allocation for you.

HOW DISCIPLINE AFFECTS RETURNS

Investing without a clear and disciplined plan can affect returns. Many people buy high and sell low, which is the opposite of what you want to do. If the market rises, investors often stay in the investment too long, hoping for more gains. If the market tanks and an investor is afraid of losing more money, they'll often sell. They buy in when the market has already had most of its growth, and when the downturn comes, they bail out at the bottom. This cycle just repeats until they lose everything.

The best long-term investors know that when there's blood in the streets, that's the best time to invest in the stock market. The point where everybody's bailing out is often the best time to buy in. After the crash of 2008, in early 2009 it was reported that Warren Buffet started making major investments, because he felt the market had gone down so much that he was bound to make a boatload more money just by picking up investments at that point. Obviously, not everybody has Warren Buffet's money, but this is an example of how the best investors come out ahead.

For most people, investing in the stock market is a prudent decision and simply needs to be part of an overall portfolio that is protected against huge losses. This can really save your bacon as you go forward in your retirement years, because it's not what you make that counts; it's what you *don't lose.* Instead of focusing on the absolute highest rates of return, it's beneficial to have a disciplined and diversified plan with a focus on avoiding the big losses.

Don't try to get your excitement out of your investments. To have an exciting life, go out and enjoy your lifestyle. If there's excitement in your investments, there will likely be disappointment as well. Instead of reaching for that shiny object and trying to earn a 15 percent rate of return, you can be happy with a lower rate of return with lower volatility and risk.

BOND INVESTMENTS

To balance the risk of an investment portfolio, the typical stockbroker-type of mentality in the past was to have

60 percent of assets in stocks and 40 percent in bonds. However, due to the diminishing performance of bonds in the recent past, this may be an antiquated approach. Investment-grade bonds once had consistent returns of 5 to 6 percent, but most bonds are nowhere near that now, due to the low-interest-rate environment. Bonds values typically fall when interest rates go up, and at the time of this writing, interest rates are rising and bond returns are very low. That makes the outlook for bonds kind of bleak.

Many investors and advisors view bonds as safer invest-ments than stocks, but I don't consider bonds to be a safety position. You can absolutely lose money in bonds. In 2008, for the first time in market history, bonds did not perform inversely to stocks. Instead, bonds sank alongside the stock market. That was not good and also not expected. It had never happened before. Now that it's happened once, could it happen again? Nobody knows that for sure, but it's important to have a strategy to protect against it. We tend to use fixed insurance contracts for the safety posi-tion instead of bonds because fixed insurance contracts are not directly impacted by interest rates. When interest rates rise—and they are definitely expected to rise—the fair market value of bonds will be pushed downward.

People invest in bonds, in part, because bonds pay divi-dends and because they want that consistent cash flow. That makes sense if you can generate the cash flow you need. However, in today's bond environment, it's unlikely the investment will perform as well as most people need it to in order to get the cash flow needed in retirement.

Additionally, if the Federal Reserve raises interest rates and hits their declared target of 2 percent, it will reduce the value of your bonds during that period if you have to sell your bond prior to maturity.

For example, let's say you have a $100,000 bond paying 4 percent interest, and you're receiving a dividend of four thousand dollars per year. It's a ten-year bond, meaning the rate of that bond is fixed for ten years.

Five years into that ten-year bond, you have an emergency and need to sell your bond. The problem is, let's assume the Fed has raised interest rates, and the current interest rate for ten-year bonds is now 5 percent. A new bond investor can take their $100,000 and receive a 5 percent rate of return, earning five thousand dollars annually for a ten-year period. It's not likely that investor would buy your bond for its face value of $100,000 since your bond earns only 4 percent interest and therefore one thousand dollars less than the current bonds earning 5 percent.

To determine the market rate of your bond in this scenario, you'd divide your current dividend (four thousand dollars) by the market interest rate (5 percent). This means your bond now has a market value of only eighty thousand dollars, which is twenty thousand dollars less than you paid for it. That's a pretty substantial loss. This is one of the reasons why we are using bond alternatives in the marketplace instead of putting money into places expected to be impacted negatively by rising interest rates. Historically, bonds have been a decent place to invest money, but we're shying away from the buy-and-hold type bonds in the current market for most investors.

Beyond interest rates, bonds can also carry additional risk. The issuing company or municipality could experience financial trouble and default on their bond commitment. Here in Rhode Island, the city of Central Falls declared bankruptcy. They had bondholders that were hurt. Puerto Rico is in a very poor position and simply doesn't have the money needed to pay their bondholders. Those bondholders will very likely lose large amounts of money. Municipalities like Detroit, and others in California, have also declared bankruptcy and defaulted on bonds. Because of the risk of bankruptcies and rising interest rates, it's difficult for me to tell a client that bonds are a safe place to put their money.

MUTUAL FUND INVESTMENTS

Many people are familiar with mutual funds, it's an investment category that can comprise many different types of investments. You can have a bond-based mutual fund or a stock-based mutual fund. With stock mutual funds, there are funds that focus on different sizes of companies (large cap, mid cap, small cap) and different objectives (like value or growth). Many mutual funds also have a blend of stocks and bonds.

I believe mutual funds can be great for people at the beginning stages of investing because one mutual fund might own anywhere from fifty to two hundred different investments. Within one mutual fund, you can achieve some diversification and reduce your risk level.

Along with mutual funds, there's another type of investment called an exchange-traded fund (ETF), and it works in a similar manner. The only technical difference between the two is that mutual funds generally have higher internal costs because of people moving in and out of the fund, and mutual funds typically have higher management fees. An advantage of an ETF is that you can liquidate it anytime throughout the day, whereas mutual fund orders are only executed at the end of the day. Therefore, ETFs are slightly more liquid as investments.

It's important to look beyond your investment statements and research your mutual funds (and other investments) to see what the actual management fees are. Our process when meeting with prospective clients is to do a full analysis of their investments and the associated fees, especially with mutual funds. Mutual funds tend to have a higher average cost within them that you don't see on the monthly statements. This is one of the reasons why we tend to prefer ETFs over mutual funds. The table on the following pages shows an example of the fee analysis that I conduct for current and prospective clients.

In the fee analysis, we list the mutual fund holdings, their historical returns, their expense ratio, and the impact of their trading costs. On that simple chart, people can often see that they are paying more expenses in their mutual funds than they expected.

In this particular example, I was able to show a prospective client that they were paying an estimated 3.83% in fees each year, through mutual fund costs, advisory fees, and variable annuity contract fees. This meant they were paying fees in the amount of $37,691.34, and they were paying this type of fee *every year*.

Another one of our clients had a mutual fund with a behind-the-scenes fee of over 2 percent per year. That is far too much to pay for mutual fund management, in my opinion. There are better ways to build a portfolio without needing to pay these high back-end expenses of mutual funds.

Fee Analysis

Expense, Performance & Morningstar Rating [1]

Date: August 29, 2017					Client Name: Mr. & Mrs. Client					Prepared By: Jeff Massey		
Name	Ticker	Total Return 1 Yr	Total Return Annlzd 5 Yr	Turnover Ratio[4]	Class Share	12 Month Yield	Standard Deviation	Prospectus Net Expense Ratio	Personal Fund Cost of Owner-ship	Total MF Exp Ratio	Mutual Fund Expense 07/31/17	Mutual Fund Valuation 08/28/17 [3]
Qualified Holdings												
AllianzGI Convertible A	ANZAX	-7.11	6.05	73%	A	1.50	10.63	0.98	1.84	1.84%	$ 104.07	$ 5,655.87
BlackRock Global Allocation Inv A	MDLOX	-3.73	3.32	84%	A	1.09	8.78	1.14	1.74	1.74%	$ 58.10	$ 3,339.09
Columbia Contrarian Core A	LCCAX	1.55	11.89	60%	A	2.48	12.94	1.09	1.84	1.84%	$ 160.58	$ 8,727.41
Columbia Strategic Income A	COSIX	2.02	4.39	169%	A	3.79	4.89	1.03	1.47	1.47%	$ 50.27	$ 3,419.57
Eaton Vance Glbl Macro Abs Ret Advtg A	EGRAX	2.97	2.86	75%	A	6.29	4.74	1.57	2.22	2.22%	$ 42.58	$ 1,918.14
Ivy Science & Technology A	WSTAX	-16.07	9.20	24%	A	0.00	15.77	1.26	1.48	1.48%	$ 54.77	$ 3,700.43
JHancock Emerging Markets A	JEVAX	-9.08	-4.54	14%	A	1.44	18.87	1.45	1.58	1.58%	$ 154.89	$ 9,803.07
JHancock Global Absolute Ret Strats A	JHAAX	-5.50	0.00	80%	A	6.90	0.00	1.63	2.31	2.31%	$ 72.10	$ 3,121.08
JPMorgan International Val A	JFEAX	-16.31	-1.77	74%	A	1.20	16.26	1.35	2.39	2.39%	$ 167.56	$ 7,011.05
JPMorgan Value Advantage A	JVAAX	-3.15	10.55	17%	A	0.59	11.83	1.25	1.43	1.43%	$ 126.24	$ 8,827.80
MFS International Growth A	MGRAX	-3.32	2.16	38%	A	0.97	14.58	1.19	1.74	1.74%	$ 108.18	$ 6,217.48
Natixis ASG Managed Futures Strategy A	AMFAX	4.02	5.08	0%	A	1.03	10.50	1.73		1.73%	$ 61.58	$ 3,559.43
Nuveen Global Infrastructure A	FGIAX	6.80	8.28	133%	A	1.78	11.46	1.22	3.26	3.26%	$ 193.21	$ 5,926.60
Oppenheimer Global Opportunities A	OPGIX	6.58	8.13	16%	A	0.11	16.97	1.19	1.50	1.50%	$ 75.94	$ 5,062.85
Prudential Jennison Natural Resources A	PGNAX	-6.81	-9.42	35%	A	0.29	25.80	1.22	1.55	1.55%	$ 62.89	$ 4,057.65
Putnam Capital Spectrum A	PVSAX	-9.21	8.45	31%	A	0.00	12.47	1.25	1.54	1.54%	$ 98.62	$ 6,404.10
Wells Fargo Core Bond A	MBFAX	5.99	3.95	586%	A	1.39	2.91	0.78	2.31	2.31%	$ 117.59	$ 5,090.67
Wells Fargo Premier Large Co Gr A	EKJAX	-5.84	8.91	44%	A	0.00	14.34	1.11	1.64	1.64%	$ 78.37	$ 4,778.66

Fee Analysis

Expense, Performance & Morningstar Rating [1]

Date: August 29, 2017 | **Client Name: Mr. & Mrs. Client** | **Prepared By: Jeff Massey**

Name	Ticker	Total Return 1 Yr	Total Return Annlzd 5 Yr	Turnover Ratio*	Class Share	12 Month Yield	Standard Deviation	Prospectus Net Expense Ratio	Personal Fund Cost of Ownership	Total MF Exp Ratio	Mutual Fund Expense 07/31/17	Mutual Fund Valuation [3] 08/28/17
Non-Qualified Holdings												
BlackRock Multi-Asset Income Investor C	BCICX	-0.02	4.57	60%	C	3.94	5.73	1.59	3.56	3.56%	$ 554.15	$ 15,565.97
Lord Abbett Multi-Asset Income C	ISFCX	-2.78	3.62	26%	C	3.05	6.93	1.92	2.26	2.26%	$ 381.04	$ 16,860.05
MFS Intl Diversification C	MDIGX	-4.95	2.04	4%	C	1.30	13.61	1.93	-	1.93%	$ 89.22	$ 4,622.95
Prudential Jennison Equity Income C	AGOCX	-1.92	7.44	76%	C	2.29	11.95	1.88	4.41	4.41%	$ 674.69	$ 15,299.16
Putnam Capital Spectrum C	PVSCX	-9.91	7.64	31%	C	0.00	12.47	2.00	3.18	3.18%	$ 288.53	$ 9,073.36
Putnam Dynamic Asset Allocation Gr C	PAECX	-3.73	6.80	196%	C	1.09	11.61	1.81	4.44	4.44%	$ 789.73	$ 17,786.81
Mutual Fund Average	-	-3.45%	5.13%	-	-	-	-	-	-	2.60%	$ 4,564.92	$ 175,829.25

	%	Cost	Portfolio Value
Mutual Fund Cost	2.60%	$4,564.92	$175,829.25
Advisory Fee			
Account Number: 4909	1.27%	$1,412.23	$111,198.92
VA Contract Costs	4.21%	$31,714.19	$753,135.13
Total Estimated Costs	**3.83%**	**$37,691.34**	**$984,256.01**

Mutual Fund Rating is Performance information obtained from Morningstar Reports, 8/10-7/31/2017

2 Mutual Fund Cost of Ownership was obtained from PersonalFund.com and based on 7/31/2017 month end data. Cost information assumed the following: A.) 25% Federal and 15% Dividends and Long Term Cap Gains; B.) 10-year holding period; C.) 17% annual return. 1 cash/1 exch. 0% Annual

Return High Yield Bond, Moderate Allocation, Is Balanced Funds, 7% Foreign Bond Fds, 9% Annual Return Bond Funds to Municipal Returns to Municipal Bond Funds. State Specific 9%

3 8/29/2017 Mutual Fund Valuations were estimated by taking number of shares held per fund, as of 7/31/2017 times fund's 8/28/2017 closing NAV.

4 Turnover Ratio is a measure of the fund's trading activity, which is computed by taking the lessor of purchase or sales (excluding all securities with maturities of less than one year) and dividing by average monthly net assets.

Information contained in this report is based on sources and data believed to be reliable, but its accuracy is not guaranteed and should not be used as such. The summary is for your information only and is not an offer or solicitation to buy or sell securities

Global Financial Private Capital is an SEC Registered Investment Adviser. Global Financial does not engage in the sale of insurance products to advisory clients. Your investment adviser representative may have a separate outside business activity as an insurance agent offering insurance. Any activity by your investment adviser representative in an insurance
agent is separate from and outside of his or her role on behalf Global Financial. You should understand the following: 1) Global Financial does not serve as an insurance agency for your investment adviser representative to offer fixed insurance; 2) Global Financial does not conduct due diligence of the fixed insurance; fixed annuities or fixed indexed annuities; 2) Global Financial does not conduct due diligence of the fixed insurance; fixed annuities or fixed indexed annuities offered
by your investment adviser representative in his or her separate capacity as an insurance agent; and 3) Global Financial does not review, approve nor supervise your investment adviser representative's recommendations as an insurance agent to hold, purchase or sell/surrender fixed insurance; fixed annuities or fixed indexed annuities. This Financial Plan is presented to illustrate a potential financial
scenario based on the information provided to Global Financial Private Capital. Global Financial accepts no responsibility for any annuity or commission product being offered.

Helping to reduce fees is part of a fiduciary duty to work in the best interest of a client. The Department of Labor has been moving toward a fiduciary standard, requiring any advisor working with your retirement accounts to work in your best interest. This is not required by law yet, but I've been a fiduciary since 2003, when I earned my professional certification as a Certified Financial Planner™. As I am an Investment Advisor Representative with AE Wealth Management, LLC, an SEC Registered Investment Advisor firm, I have a statutory requirement to work as a fiduciary. Obviously, I think it's very important to work in our clients' best interest at all times. Identifying and reducing investment management fees is just one part of the fiduciary duty we owe our clients.

RETIREMENT PLAN STRUCTURES

Let's talk a bit more about retirement plans, which may take the form of an Individual Retirement Arrangement (IRA) or another structure you may have through your employer, such as a 401(k), 403(b), or 457 plan.

IRAS (INDIVIDUAL RETIREMENT ARRANGEMENT)

The IRA account structure was created in 1974, and there are currently many different types of IRAs: Simple IRAs, SEP IRAs, Traditional IRAs, and Roth IRAs. Each type has somewhat different rules that you should be aware of.

To build and maintain my knowledge of IRA regulations, I receive specialized training with the Ed Slott organization out of New York. Ed is a CPA, a top-level advisor, and an expert in the field who is consistently quoted in the *Wall Street Journal* and many other financial publications. I am a member of his Master Elite IRA Advisor program,[1] and have been involved with his organization for over seven years. We attend training two times per year that is focused on IRAs and retirement plans. It's a bit expensive, but I take it very seriously because I want to make sure I'm on top of the game when it comes to providing the best advice to my clients. There are only about four hundred advisors in the entire country who have received this specialized level of training through the Ed Slott organization.[2]

In 2017, people under the age of fifty could contribute up to $5,500 to an IRA per year. If you're age fifty or better, you could add another $1,000 in IRA contributions for a total of $6,500 per year. If you're contributing to a Traditional IRA, you might be able to deduct your contribution, depending on your total income and whether you have a retirement plan at work. You must have earned income of at least $5,500 (or $6,500 if you are age fifty or above) to

---

1   Ed Slott's Elite IRA Advisor Group ("Ed Slott") is a membership organization. Qualifying criteria include payment of annual dues and attendance of workshops. Membership with Ed Slott in no way implies that Jeffrey H. Massey is an IRA distribution expert. Ed Slott is not affiliated with Massey & Associates, Inc.

2   "Elite IRA Consumer Group Consumer Page," IRAHelp.com, https://www.irahelp.com/about-ed-slotts-elite-ira-advisor-group.

contribute the maximum amount. As long as one spouse has enough earnings, both can contribute up to the maximum amount.

If you and your spouse both have retirement plans at work, the tax deduction for contributions begins to be phased out if you have $99,000 or more in adjusted gross income, and it's totally phased out if you have $119,000 or more in adjusted gross income for 2017. If only one of the spouses has a retirement plan at work, those numbers jump dramatically to $186,000 to begin to phase out and $196,000 for the total phase-out. These dollar amounts change annually, so check the amount for the tax year you're working with.

For many people, the IRA contribution of $5,500 or $6,500 is very viable, and it's important to do that. The younger you start that, the better off you will be at retirement. An IRA is not an investment, but a tax structure and method of holding the investment assets. Think of the IRA as a bucket in which you can put many different types of investments: bank CDs, money market accounts, stocks, bonds, mutual funds, exchange traded funds, annuity contracts, and more.

One big advantage of a SEP IRA is that it's similar to a pension plan in the higher amount that you can contribute each year. In 2017 you could contribute up to 25 percent of your net business income into a SEP IRA, or a maximum of $54,000. That's a huge amount of money, although you'd need a net business income over $200,000 per year to have a contribution that high.

401(K) PLANS

In 1978 Congress created a rule to allow people to make pretax contributions to 401(k) plans. With 401(k) plans, people under fifty years old can currently put a maximum of $18,000 in earned income into their retirement plan. If they're over fifty years old, they can add $6,000 more for a total maximum contribution of $24,000. However, the employer can also add money to those retirement accounts. For people over the age of fifty, as of 2017, the employer can add up to $30,000 more for a total annual maximum of $54,000.

It's also important to note your deductible IRA contributions must be during a year when you have earned income. If you're retired and only earning income from your investments, you can't contribute to an IRA and deduct it from your taxes.

Some people ask whether they should convert their Traditional IRA to a Roth IRA. My general advice is that the younger you are, the better off you are with a Roth IRA or a 401(k) Roth. Again, my opinion is that tax rates will likely increase because of the federal government's growing expenses and deficit. I do not believe we can grow the economy fast enough to pay that down, and additional tax revenue will be needed in the future. With a Roth IRA, you pay today's tax rates on your contributions, your investments grow without taxation, and you can begin to receive the growth of the account at age fifty-nine-and-a-half or beyond, income tax-free. This assumes you play by the rules, of course.

The rules are that the Roth IRA must have been in place for five years and that you are age fifty-nine and one half (or older). By the way, the five-year rule must be complied with, even *after* your death, in order for the growth to come out of the Roth IRA account income-tax-free. If you set up a Roth IRA, then passed away three years later, your heirs would have to wait two more years before they could withdraw the growth without income taxation. Contribution and converted dollars can be withdrawn prior to the five-year requirement because the taxes were already paid on those dollars.

I believe you should take advantage of a Roth IRA while you still can. Roth IRAs have recently been in the crosshairs of the government. They are looking at the possibility of taking away the favorable tax treatment of Roth IRAs. It's been shot down thus far, but as things get tighter economically, there's an increasing possibility that Roth IRAs may be discontinued.

INVESTMENT RISKS

We've touched on a few common risks in regard to retirement investments, from the risk of stock market losses to the risk of rising interest rates and issuer bankruptcies in the bond market. There are a handful of other risks that you do not want to ignore when evaluating and reviewing your investments.

INFLATION

Inflation happens when there's a rise in the price of goods or services over the course of time. Most of us are familiar with inflation, as many of our common expenditures rise consistently in price over time.

When I was a young kid, I had a job pumping gas at a local gas station. I remember the price of gas back then: thirty-six cents per gallon. This fact dates me a bit, but the rise in the cost of gasoline is an everyday example of inflation. It's important to have your portfolio structured so you've got enough growth to retain the purchasing power you need for your expenses in retirement.

As of 2017, the rate of inflation has been tame over the last several years, thankfully. It's hovered around 2 percent per year, depending on which inflationary index you're looking at. To mitigate the risk of inflation, keep an eye on the increasing costs of the goods and services important to you in retirement and plan accordingly.

EXCESSIVE FEES

In our earlier discussion of mutual funds, I mentioned the risk of excessive fees. This risk applies to all of your investments, and it also applies to the fees charged by your advisors. We've seen advisory fees of 2 percent to 3 percent, which is more than you need to pay to receive quality fiduciary-level planning in your best interest. You don't need to spend that much money on an annual basis.

Recently we've seen variable annuities with, in my opinion, some absolutely insane management fees, with one annuity in particular charging an annual fee of 4.21 percent. That particular client had $753,000 in variable annuities and was paying over $31,000 per year in fees! That is simply outrageous. Think about that for a moment: $31,000 per year means that over the ten-year term of that contract, he would have paid over $310,000 in fees! This is why you need to be aware of all the various fees within your investments, and it's why we expose these fees as part of our very detailed analysis for current and prospective clients.

Sometimes fees are worth paying. When we identify the management fees within a client's investment—whether it's a mutual fund, variable annuity, or any other investment—we ask if the benefits of that investment are worth the fees. In some cases, that answer may be yes. That's a case-by-case situation, and it's different for everybody. We simply look at each investment's fees and make the best recommendation that we can. There are times when, even with the same couple, we say, "Look, this one you should keep, this one is garbage, and you should make some changes to this one."

Excessive fees can be harmful to the long-term growth of an investment. You'll want to ask your advisors to be transparent and show you what your investment fee structure will be because it is a big factor into the growth of your investments moving forward.

CHURNING

Churning happens when an advisor or stockbroker encourages excessive buying and selling of investments, to generate a commission for the advisor. This normally takes the form of a broker frequently telling you to sell one of your stocks or bonds to buy other stocks and bonds. This could be considered churning, if they're doing that too often.

If that's going on with your account, ask them the question, "Why are you recommending this investment? Is it really that much better? Am I really going to benefit that much by selling my investment and buying the new one you're recommending?"

The other question I'd ask is whether they are a fiduciary advisor. If they're working for a wire house or stock brokerage firm, it's less likely they are fiduciary advisors. You want to work with fiduciaries who will put your interests ahead of their own or that of their firm. Keep in mind that in publicly-traded brokerage firms, the company works in the interest of the shareholders. The job of the company is to enhance the value of the company for the shareholders. Can they really put your interests first?

HEALTHCARE EXPENSES

We cannot ignore the current and future impact of healthcare expenses. Fidelity released surveys estimating that the average sixty-five-year-old couple may spend over $250,000 on healthcare expenses in their remaining years of life.[3]

To make matters worse, what if you need living assistance or long-term care? You'll either need to pay for a professional to come into your home to care for you, or you'll

---

3   "Health Care Costs for Couples in Retirement Rise to an Estimated $260,000, Fidelity Analysis Shows," Fidelity Investments, August 16, 2016, https://www.fidelity.com/about-fidelity/employer-services/health-care-costs-for-couples-in-retirement-rise.

have to transition into an assisted living facility. The average home healthcare provider in Rhode Island currently charges between twenty dollars and twenty-five dollars per hour. Assisted living facilities range from $4,500 to $10,000 per *month*. Now you're talking about some very serious dollars in a short period of time.[4]

The risk of some healthcare expenses can be transferred to an insurance company, and in many cases, it's prudent to do that. Just as you have homeowner's insurance to reimburse you if your house burns down, or car insurance to protect the value of your car, there are insurance products that protect your retirement savings from being drained by long-term care expenses. There are many different products and strategies toward this type of protection, and it's something you'd want to talk about with your trusted advisor as we do with our clients. It's important to discuss the features and benefits of the main two different product types. First is the traditional type of coverage, where you buy a monthly benefit dollar amount for a period of years. An example would be $250 daily benefit for three years of coverage.

Secondly, there are the hybrid-type long-term care plans. These are life insurance policies that have built in long-term care benefit features. There are many different types

---

4   "Cost of Care," Genworth Financial, Inc., https://www.genworth.com/about-us/industry-expertise/cost-of-care.html.

of hybrid policies. One example would be if you had a life insurance policy paying a death benefit of $200,000, you can draw down from the death benefit to help you with your long-term care expenses. There are many choices, and this is just an example of how one might work. I always suggest that you work with a fiduciary who has your best interest ahead of their own to determine which type of long-term care product would be the best fit for you.

SUMMARY

Several different types of risks can impact how you're going to do financially in your retirement years, and each type of investment carries its own type of risks. It's important to understand those risks and then to diversify your portfolio to protect your assets.

Measure each of your investments using the criteria of safety, liquidity, and growth potential. Remember, you normally will only get to have two of those elements in any one investment. It's important to diversify across different types of investments to ensure you have your preferred levels of safety, liquidity, and growth potential within your entire portfolio. My bias and focus is to avoid big losses in the worst economic downturns. If you can avoid those big hits, you'll be in a better position over time.

Remember, it's not how much you make, it's how much

you *don't lose.* As you move into your retirement years, avoiding loss and enabling the continued growth of your investments can make a positive and impactful difference for you.

Certainty of Income

The foundation of retirement planning is determining the amount of income you need to generate to live comfortably in your retirement years. The amount of income you'll need in retirement will be driven by your lifestyle.

To determine what your lifestyle needs will be in retirement, I ask my clients, "What is your lifestyle costing you today?" After I ask that question, it's quite interesting to see the looks I get on people's faces. In most cases, they have absolutely no clue what their lifestyle costs are.

A few years ago, I met with a couple. The husband was an engineer, and when I started to fill out a simple income and expense sheet to begin their planning, he stopped me. "Oh no," he said. "You don't need to do that. I already know our numbers on this. We spend about four thousand dollars per month on living expenses."

I believed him, because he was the one who paid the bills each month. Plus, he was an engineer, after all! Nevertheless, just to be sure they would have no surprises in their retirement, I replied, "Great, that sounds like a pretty fair number. Let's just take a few to minutes to double-check that."

To quickly determine your income and expenses, you can total up the income and expense totals on twelve of your monthly bank statements and divide those numbers by twelve. That's what I did for this couple, with the intent that we would then move on to look at their retirement income (social security, pension, investments) and see if their income would cover their expenses.

When we totaled up the actual expenses for the past twelve months, it wasn't $4,000 per month. It was *$6,000* per month. I was shocked. "Well," he said, "it looks like I was wrong." It was a huge underestimation of their expenses, and unfortunately, I see this often.

Understanding your expenses is critical to your retirement planning, and it only takes about fifteen minutes to find this information from your bank statements. It takes less time to calculate that number than it takes to go to the grocery store. It's the foundation of your retirement plan because if you can't generate enough income to sustain your lifestyle, something needs to change. You may need to work longer than you'd anticipated or trim your expenses or figure out a way to supplement your income to have the money you need for living expenses during your retirement years.

FOCUS ON NET INCOME

We all have a gross income, but we've got to focus on our net income when planning for retirement because those are the dollars you get to spend. Earning $80,000 a year may only net you $65,000 of spendable money. In your retirement planning, you'll want to do this same calculation to account for federal and state income taxes (if applicable) to determine the amount of money you'll be able to spend.

Thankfully, many of our clients drop down into a lower tax bracket in their retirement years. Often, clients' working income will put them in a 25 percent income tax bracket (or higher), but their retirement income drops them down to a 15 percent tax bracket. That's a huge savings on tax expenditures when it happens.

When determining if clients will have enough net income to cover their needs in retirement, it's important for me to understand the full amount of income they expect to come in, as well as understand what type of income it will be. Will the income stream be coming from Social Security? Is there any income from a pension fund? Will you or your spouse be earning income from working part time? As one might imagine, there are many different details that can go into a person's unique retirement planning.

ANALYSIS AND TECHNOLOGY

At our firm, we utilize cutting-edge technology to ensure we consider as many different scenarios as possible in a client's income planning for retirement. With the Massey On Money™ Retirement Roadmap, we use innovative software programs to answer questions such as:

- Based on your current level of risk, how might your retirement income be affected if the stock market were to decline slightly, moderately, or severely?
- At what point is it possible that you will run out of money? What possible scenarios could accelerate this or prevent this?

Let's look at how we would conduct analysis to find the answers to both of those questions. Based on current trends in the marketplace, we'll use our software to apply a conservative rate of growth to your portfolio of investments. We'll also account for the expected rate of inflation to illustrate the true purchasing power of your income in the future.

It's common for people to focus on the optimistic assumptions and scenarios when it comes to their retirement income. If our software and analysis shows the possibility of income lasting to the age of ninety-three years old, for example, it's common for a client to say, "Great, I'm okay with that. I'm never going to make it to that age."

"Okay, that's fine," I might reply. "But what if we have another stock market meltdown and you have a high percentage of your holdings in the stock market. What's that going to do to your income?" After asking that question, I'll then use the software to show the possible impact of a severe stock market meltdown to the client's future retirement income. Suddenly, the income that may have lasted until age ninety-three might now run out a decade earlier, at the age of eighty-three.

Seeing the contrast between these two scenarios helps in evaluating the various approaches we could take. If a client wants to minimize the impact of another stock market meltdown (like the one we experienced in 2008), then they'll want to build some safety into their overall portfolio. I believe it's a significant consideration for retirees, and these scenarios should be examined in the same way an electrocardiogram (EKG) would be viewed in determining the health of your heart. You want to examine the red line that indicates where you can expect difficulties.

To determine where the points of difficulty might be within a client's future income, we use our software to perform what we refer to as a stress test. This is very similar to the stress tests performed by federal regulators to assess risk levels in the banking industry. If a major bank wishes to pay a dividend to its shareholders, that distribution of cash (which could otherwise be held as a cash reserve) could present a risk to the bank's ability to weather economic downturns. Because of this, the federal regulators will perform a stress test to determine whether a dividend payment can be permitted. A few years ago, the regulators' stress test determined that Bank of America should not and could not pay a dividend to shareholders, and the bank was forced to readjust their investments to be more conservative before they would be permitted to distribute the dividend they desired.

We have similar software and provide the same type of stress testing for our clients. Instead of looking at the past through the rearview mirror, we'll look through the windshield of the car to see what might be coming next. If the stock market crashes, what might that do to your investments? What if interest rates continue to climb? What if China's economy continues to slow down? We can even run scenarios based on political considerations. How might each of those scenarios impact your current holdings?

With our software, we can simulate over sixty different scenarios to help our clients look through their windshield to anticipate the impact of various events on their retirement income plan. One of the significant advantages to working with a professional advisor who specializes in retirement planning is that you'll often have access to this type of stress-testing software. This software and service helps you build a plan that enables you to feel a higher level of confidence and certainty regarding your future income in retirement. In essence, you're looking through the windshield instead of the rearview mirror. Many advisors will show you the average rate of return for various investments over various periods of time, perhaps five years or ten years. That, to me, is looking in the rearview mirror when you're driving down the highway! Not likely to have a good outcome.

Many of our clients decide they'd like to have at least some of their retirement income guaranteed by using products backed up by the claims-paying ability of an insurance company. Some people don't utilize those types of products, however, because everyone's needs and goals are different. It's important to work with an advisor who isn't pigeonholed into one option. If you work with an advisor who only deals with insurance products, or with an investment broker who only invests in the stock market, you'll be missing the opportunity to incorporate the full range of solutions that can be seamlessly incorporated together to accomplish your goals.

BENEFITS OF STRESS TESTS

Identifying the worst-case scenario is a huge benefit of stress testing your investment portfolio. The most recent worst-case scenario would be the 2008 stock market crash when the market fell by 37 percent.

Our stress test software replicates what happened in 2008 and applies the same outcome to your portfolio. The software will show the impact on your current investments if 2008 happened again in the stock market. Most of the analysis we have done on portfolios over the last couple of years shows that many investors would suffer losses in the range of *30 to 40 percent*. People with riskier or more aggressive portfolios could be exposed to losses of *50 percent or more*. The absolute worst stress test result showed a possible loss of *62 percent*. Needless to say, that is a staggering level of risk and would likely disrupt their retirement plans.

Some people know they're taking a lot of risk. A gentleman who came in for a meeting recently told me up front that he knew his investments were too aggressive and that he held over $1.5 million in only six different investments. It was no surprise to him when we showed him the results of his stress test, showing the potential for very heavy losses in the future if the market crash of 2008 happened again.

Most people I've worked with are not like that gentleman. Most people are in complete shock after we conduct the stress test and they see they could lose 30 to 40 percent of their money. They are not happy with the level of risk they find themselves in. It's not uncommon for one spouse to look at the other and say, "What? We told our advisor we didn't want that much risk!" Yet that's exactly what they have in their portfolio.

In a situation like that, we'll first look at all the ways we can reduce their exposure to the risk of loss. Commonly, a couple's next concern is whether their income will last for both of their lifetimes. That might lead into a conversation about fixed-index annuities, which tend to work well for many situations. There are different categories of these types of annuities. Some annuities are what I call accumulation vehicles, having no fees on an annual basis and no extra bells and whistles. These are an easy way to share in the growth of the stock market while avoiding its losses. If the market goes down, you won't receive any interest credits, but you'll also avoid losing money. Any previously credited interest will remain in the contract. Due to this feature, this type of annuity can often provide a nice balance in a client's portfolio, and serve as an alternative to bonds.

For people who are less concerned about accumulating dollars and more concerned about generating a guaranteed income stream, there are products that can serve that need. The income payout could begin the next month or could be deferred to begin in one year or deferred to begin ten or twenty years down the road. There are many different types of these products out there (from many different companies), but let's take a look at how they work in general.

Generally, this type of annuity would have an income rider fee around 1 percent, on average. Some might be a little less or a little more, but 1 percent is a good assumption for this example. You'll pay the 1 percent annually, in exchange for an annuity contract with a highly rated insurance company. The insurance company will then add a fixed percentage to your income account value each year. Contracts differ, but most will "roll up" like this for ten years. Some contracts are less than ten years, and some go out to twenty years. The roll-up feature continues until you begin taking your income payments.

Let's say that your annuity begins with a balance of $100,000 and the insurance company has guaranteed to add 6 percent to that $100,000 each year for a period of five years. At the end of the five years, you'll determine how you'd like to take the payout.

Again, products differ, but most contracts will allow for a single-life payout or a joint-life payout for a husband and wife. These payments, if you play by the rules, will be guaranteed by the insurance company based on their claims-paying ability.

Many of these types of contracts are also flexible in terms of allowing you to change when you'd like to begin taking your payments. If you decide you want to take your payments after ten years of growth instead of five years of growth, it's possible to have that type of flexibility in many annuity contracts.

If your original $100,000 rolled up at the rate of 6 percent in the income account for five years, you would end that five-year period with a little over $133,000 in income account value. This income account value will be used solely to generate your income payments. It is not a value that you can receive in a lump-sum payment. Each company has determined a payout percentage based on age and (in some cases) gender. If that calculation determines the insurance company will pay you 5 percent of your income account value annually, then you'll receive nearly $6,700 every year for the remainder of your life, even if the account value of the base annuity contract goes down to zero. This is a huge benefit that guarantees your income will last as long as you do.

The cool part about these types of annuities is that if you live a very long time, you can receive much more money than you paid in because they'll continue to pay you for the rest of your life. If you start at age sixty-five and live to be one hundred and five, you'll receive payments for forty years. Some of these contracts offer a joint-life payout, guaranteeing an income for the life of *both* spouses. If you're married and not too far apart in age, then a joint payout can often make sense in ensuring that both of you will have an income for life. Unfortunately, should you choose to receive income for life instead of a specified period of time, any remaining value in the annuity upon a premature death will be retained by the insurance company.

Some types of annuity contracts also have features that provide additional money to pay for long-term care expenses. For example, in a small number of contracts, if your health starts failing and you need help with two of out six activities of daily living (bathing, eating, dressing, toileting, transferring, and maintaining continence), the insurance company will take your $6,700 and double that payment for a maximum of up to five years if you qualify each year. In that case, you would receive annual payments of $13,400 for up to five years. There aren't many contracts that offer that benefit, but in the policies that do, it may make sense to take advantage of them. Please know, however, that these increased income payments will accelerate the depreciation of the base annuity's account value.

This illustration is for informational purposes and intended only to demonstrate how a hypothetical fixed-index annuity might have performed based on the stated assumptions. This illustration does not represent any specific product. Annuities are insurance products that may be subject to restrictions, surrender charges, and holding periods, which vary by carrier. Riders are generally optional and have an additional associated cost. Annuities are not bank or FDIC insured.

Fixed-index annuities are not a direct investment in the stock market. They are long-term insurance products with guarantees backed by the financial strength and claims-paying ability of the issuing company. They provide the potential for interest to be credited based in part on the performance of specific indexes without the risk of loss of premium due to market downturns or fluctuation. They may not be appropriate for everyone.

When researching options for our clients, we find the three best products that suit their needs. We gather all the parameters of each individual's situation—including the age of the client and when they anticipate needing their income—and we find the top three products available for them in their resident state. In doing that, we are fulfilling our fiduciary duty to find the best products out there for the client's particular situation. That's what being a fiduciary is all about: finding the best product for a client's needs, instead of just selling one company's product to all clients.

If you're working with someone who is a captive agent, it's highly possible that their company may not have the best product in all of the categories you need help with. At our firm, we're not captive agents. We are independent fiduciary advisors, and we have access to a much wider array of products and companies compared to someone that only sells one company's products. This allows us to provide you with our best recommendation possible after analyzing hundreds of products to find the top three for your needs. We then will sit down and go over the differences between those options and allow you to make the choice you're most comfortable with.

Annuities are only the tip of the iceberg when it comes to the multitude of options that can be pursued to accomplish your goals in retirement income planning. Everybody's situation is different, and that's why you want to work with an independent fiduciary advisor who has access to a wide array of solutions to meet your needs. When your head hits the pillow at night, you want to know that you've got a plan in place that will provide you with an income for the rest of your life.

NEXT STEP: ESTIMATE INCOME AND EXPENSES

A great first step in your retirement planning is to take a few minutes to estimate your income and expenses. This is the most crucial part of your entire plan, and it will help you understand how much money you need to generate to retire comfortably.

Luckily, this exercise is one of the fastest parts of your planning process. Most of my clients tell me it takes them fifteen minutes or less to get this information from their bank statements. After you have this information in hand, it then becomes possible for your advisor to structure a plan to generate the cash flow you need. Additionally, an experienced advisor can make the necessary adjustments in your plan to account for inflation, which will help you preserve your purchasing power over time.

For the readers of this book, I've provided a downloadable version of the exact income and expense document I use with each of my clients in their retirement planning. To begin this important first step in your retirement planning, visit www.masseyandassociates.com/expenses to download the document and get started.

OPTIMIZING INCOME

When planning for the future, most of my clients want to maximize not only their incomes in retirement but also their assets to provide the best possible outcome for their heirs. To accomplish this objective, we create a plan that I refer to as a "Leveraged Legacy Plan™."

A Leveraged Legacy Plan™ is for people who may have specific objectives or needs in the transfer of their assets to the next generation or for those who simply desire to maximize the amount of money passed on to their family or charities.

Everyone's situation is different, however, and the key to this planning is finding the scenario that maximizes your assets and transfers them in the most tax-efficient manner possible to your heirs.

AVOIDING LOSS

My bias, again, is to protect against the downsides and avoid financial losses when helping clients achieve their goals. With that in mind, our leveraged legacy programs consist of products whose performance is guaranteed by the underwriting insurance company. We often use fixed annuities that guarantee a certain payment each year. Often, that contract is structured to provide payments until the second spouse passes away.

The life insurance policies we use have premiums that are fixed and guaranteed not to rise. The policies are funded with the guaranteed cash flow of the fixed annuities, and the life insurance death benefits are typically guaranteed to the age of 121 years old. As of the time of this writing, nobody in America has lived to be 121 years old, so we're confident these policies will be in place for a client's lifetime.

The guarantees of these insurance products are backed up by the claims-paying ability of the insurance carriers. Please keep in mind that AE Wealth Management, LLC, is not affiliated with any insurance company or products that are being discussed in this book.

This is why we like to use a blend of insurance products in our leveraged legacy planning instead of taking a flier on a risky stock and hoping it produces a big financial result. We like to use a guaranteed fixed annuity to fund a life insurance plan with guaranteed premiums and a guaranteed death benefit. Locking in all of these valuable guarantees helps in providing value to our clients while reducing the risk of financial loss.

There is a wide variety of insurance products and functions, and insurance can be very complicated. When I hear somebody say they don't like life insurance in any form, it almost makes me chuckle a bit internally. A blanket statement like that indicates a lack of understanding toward the many different functions of life insurance contracts, and the wide range of objectives that can be achieved through the usage of life insurance.

On the technical side of leveraged legacy planning, it's possible to structure a plan in a way that it will not increase the taxable value of your estate upon your death. This type of planning is more technical and involves the appropriate implementation of specific legal documents. It's crucially important to have these legal documents in place, and it can be very problematic for you and your beneficiaries if any legal issues are overlooked in your legal documentation and structuring. In the next chapter, we'll look at the importance of legal documents in your planning and working with an estate planning attorney.

CHAPTER

Legal Documents: Ignore at Your Own Peril

It's possible to do everything right when it comes to retirement planning yet ruin everything with a lack of proper legal planning. If you ignore this area entirely or simply don't execute your legal documents properly, the Internal Revenue Service might be the inheritor of the money you'd intended for your family or charities. Most of my clients prefer to maximize the value of the assets they leave to their children and grandchildren and minimize the amount of estate taxes that need to be paid to Uncle Sam at the federal and state level.

As we discuss legal structures and documents in this chapter, let me be clear that I am a Certified Financial Planner™, but I am not an attorney. For my clients' legal planning, primarily, I work hand-in-hand with Mr. Paul Brule, an elder law attorney I highly respect. Paul and I have worked together for decades, and we're very like-minded. We want to make sure our clients' plans and documents are properly structured for their needs. It's critical for people to have their legal documents in order, and when I meet anyone who doesn't currently have an attorney for elder law or estate planning services, I refer them to Paul.

As a financial planning professional, I ask my clients to bring their legal documents to our initial meetings (if they have legal documents). While I am not an attorney, Paul has taught me about certain issues to look for, especially if documents come from particular law firms or lawyers we've had experience with in the past.

I'm often surprised by what I see in people's legal documents, especially when it comes to naming the person or people who will take over if you're disabled. Most often, spouses choose the other spouse to take over, but in many cases, that's where it ends, and no one else is designated as a backup. I remember one couple who had named each other but nobody beyond that. The first paragraph of their legal document mentioned their five children.

"Do you get along with your children?" I asked them.

"Well, of course!" they replied. "We get along with all of them."

"I'm curious, then, why none of them are listed as backups to take over if you're disabled?" I asked.

For example, it would be possible for a married couple to be in a car wreck where one spouse dies, and the other ends up disabled in the hospital. If something like this were to happen, you'd want to appoint one child (or a combination of children working together) as your attorney-in-fact, empowered to make decisions to handle your financial affairs and your healthcare decisions to keep you well.

One important factor to understand is that the person you name to be your attorney-in-fact is not legally required to accept the role and do any work for you. They're allowed to sign a note that says they do not wish to take on any responsibilities as your attorney-in-fact, and effectively resign from the position. In the event that happens, it's helpful to have another person named as a backup. My attorney hammers this concept into me all the time: it is so important to have a backup person, and a backup to that person. If you have multiple children, Mr. Brule suggests that you layer multiple children within the legal documents to take over if one of the children chooses not to take on the responsibility or is unable to handle your legal or healthcare decisions.

As I've previously mentioned, I have a bias toward preserving people's assets and avoiding big losses in their financial planning. When it comes to legal documents, I have the same bias. I strongly advise against trying to create legal documents and structures on your own or through some type of fill-in-the-blank form. I believe it's critically important to meet with a qualified and experienced elder law attorney or estate planning attorney for your legal advice. This is what they specialize in, unlike a more generalized attorney who does personal injury one day, divorce the next, and estate planning every now and then. It's my opinion that you should work with a specialist to help you with your estate planning documents, not a generalist. You could search online for elder law or estate planning attorneys in your area and would likely find several qualified experts nearby.

TRUSTS

Next, I'd like to discuss the various legal documents that may provide value for you when working with elder law attorneys and estate planning attorneys. This chapter has been reviewed by my estate planning attorney to ensure everything being discussed is accurate at the time of this writing.

Firstly, there are three categories of people in a trust:

- Grantor(s), who create the trust
- Trustee(s), who control the trust
- Beneficiaries, who benefit from the trust

Generally, the grantors are usually the initial trustees in a revocable trust. Revocable means that you can make changes to the trust at any time until you pass away. As a simple example, you and your spouse could create the trust, control the assets held by the trust, and distribute money to yourselves as the initial beneficiaries.

For many people, trusts can be an effective tool in their planning. Think of a trust as a bucket in which you can hold your assets. Your trust can hold and own any type of asset (as long as it is legal), such as a savings account, checking account, money market account, mutual fund, share of stock, exchange-traded fund, or bond. One type of asset that you shouldn't put into your trust is your qualified money (such as IRAs and retirement plans) as that would cause a taxable event.

There are two main categories of trusts: revocable and irrevocable. A revocable trust can be changed anytime before your death, whereas an irrevocable trust can't be modified as you move forward. I've been in some seminars where attorneys claim to have a way to change the terms of irrevocable trusts, but I don't want to go down what I think is a dangerous path. That type of trust is classified as "irrevocable" for a reason, and it shouldn't be changed. The grantor (the creator of the trust) should feel confident that their trust will operate as expected, and it's not something that should be changed, in my opinion. Again, I am not an attorney, and you should work with a qualified estate planning attorney with these types of documents.

There are many different reasons why you might use an irrevocable trust, although we won't be focusing on most of those scenarios in this book. The one scenario that I do see often, however, involves planning for Medicaid. This is currently a highly contentious area, and it comes up for discussion every two years during the ethics training sessions I attend as a Certified Financial Planner™. The question often asked is, "Should we, as CFP®s, be involved with Medicaid planning and help people qualify to have the state pay for their nursing care?"

In the current state of the industry, it seems to be a fifty-fifty split among advisors in terms of how this question should be answered. Half feel that advisors should help their clients qualify for Medicaid; half feel we should not. The answer to that question is a personal one and not a uniform answer that this book should attempt to give you. My point in bringing this up is simply to help people understand that there is a very strong difference of opinion among financial advisors when it comes to the issue of qualifying for Medicaid to have the state pay for your nursing home expenses while you have hundreds of thousands of assets that could be used to pay for your medical care.

If you have that type of scenario brewing in your family—where one of your loved ones may be entering, or is already in, a nursing home—I would highly advise working with a financial advisor and attorney who are familiar with the rules of Medicaid. This is where an elder law attorney experienced with this part of the legal code can be of great assistance, because it is very complex and tricky. With a solid and structured plan, however, elder law attorneys could potentially save your family an enormous amount of money. I've seen case after case of families who have saved hundreds of thousands of dollars through this type of planning. Qualifying for Medicaid benefits can have a huge financial upside for a family. It carries a downside, however, for the taxpayers required to fund Medicaid and the benefits provided by the program.

My stance on the Medicaid issue is this: as a financial advisor, people come to me to create and execute a plan that helps them protect their assets from Medicaid spend-down requirements. The state government makes the rules, and it's my job to understand these rules and max-imize my clients' benefits in a way that follows the rules. As long as we're complying with the rules established by the state, I'm happy to help with this type of planning along with my attorney.

REVOCABLE TRUSTS

For most clients and their objectives, a revocable trust will be the type of trust implemented in their planning. A revocable trust is called an inter vivos trust. Inter vivos means "between the living" and an inter vivos trust is more commonly known as a living trust. This type of trust offers a high level of flexibility to the grantor, who is the person who creates it and is commonly the initial trustee and beneficiary as well.

In many cases, my clients who create these trusts end up serving all three roles: grantor, trustee, and beneficiary. They oversee the trust as a trustee, and they also receive the trust's benefits as the beneficiary. It's very common for people to set up a trust to hold their real estate assets. It could be their primary residence, rental properties, commercial property, raw land, or any other type of titled property they wish to transfer into their trust. There are no limitations as to the real estate assets they add to or remove from their revocable trust. Your retirement assets in the form of qualified money are not likely to be a good fit for a revocable trust because they lose their tax-deferred advantages. Retitling the ownership of your IRA (to the name of the trust) will make your IRA fully taxable in that tax year. Obviously, not a good idea!

A trust can be a very useful tool. One primary benefit of using a trust is the avoidance of probate court. People die, but a trust does not, and trusts therefore bypass probate court. As a result, the transition of your assets upon death happens much faster and more privately. Without a trust, if your assets must proceed through probate court proceedings, the proceedings will be public. In Rhode Island, probate court proceedings take six months or more to complete, and my attorney has told me stories of people spending years in probate court due to families fighting. A revocable trust can serve as a very important document for the ownership of your assets, especially if you'd like those assets to transfer without the necessity of probate court.

There are also many other reasons to employ a revocable trust in your planning. Trusts can allow you to create special rules regarding access to your assets. What if you have challenges with your kids or grandchildren? Along with my colleague Paul Brule, the elder law attorney, I've seen many scenarios where a trust needed to be created to handle unique challenges within a family. The challenges might range from caring for an heir with medical special needs or any situation requiring extra protection of your assets. Similar to Medicaid planning, there could be a goal of shifting assets in order to qualify for different types of government benefits.

In our contemporary society, it can be the case that heirs are simply not good with money, and trusts can be designed to prevent people from spending their money too quickly by structuring the payments to the heirs over a long period of time. Similarly, there can be more serious issues to build trusts around, such as alcoholism, drug abuse, or criminal behavior. A trust can be structured to avoid distributing a large lump sum of money to an adult child to prevent them from doing bad things or hurting themselves with a windfall of money (especially adult children with addiction problems).

A trust can also be useful if your heirs, such as grand-children, are still minors. In that case, the trust can have language for the trustees to maintain control of the assets until the grandchildren attain a certain age. That age is totally up to you—you can stipulate any age you feel it would be appropriate for them to take over the assets. I have one client who listed his two grandsons as beneficiaries, but they don't get the money until they turn sixty-two! That is a bit extreme in my opinion, but that is his choice to make, not mine.

It's possible for someone to structure a trust to provide heirs with smaller distributions of money over the course of months, years, or even decades. Smaller distributions of money can be paid out on a monthly basis for the beneficiaries' day-to-day expenses, but larger sums of money can be withheld in order to protect them from themselves. That's an important feature of a revocable trust. You can also structure an inheritance around certain milestones or actions achieved by your beneficiaries. You are allowed to structure your trust payout any way that you see fit, as long as it's legal. You can't require them to rob a bank to get their inheritance or do anything else that is illegal.

LAST WILL AND TESTAMENT

The primary purpose of a trust is to avoid the process of proving your last will and testament in probate court. Having your assets owned by a trust will help you avoid probate court, but it's still beneficial to have a last will and testament. This helps to give instructions regarding your trusts and assets.

For example, it would be easy to overlook something as simple as a bank account held in your name alone. This is a common scenario. Perhaps you were at the bank and wanted to do a bank account in both your name and your spouse's name, but your spouse wasn't able to make it, so you put it in your name and planned to fill out the necessary forms later to convert the account into joint ownership.

What happens if you pass away before your spouse is named jointly on the bank account or listed as a beneficiary? Now you have an asset in one person's name with no beneficiary listed. This is the type of situation served by probate court and a last will and testament. Your last will and testament would give the instructions that any assets overlooked upon your death should be transferred into your revocable trust after going through the necessary probate process. After approval from the probate court, the bank account would be transferred into the ownership of the trust.

A last will and testament can empower the executor of an estate in many situations involving the settling of an estate. For example, an executor could handle the deceased person's tax returns or file a lawsuit on behalf of a person's estate if they were killed in an accident involving another person's negligence. Those types of powers are granted through the probate process. You don't get those powers through the living trust.

If you have minor children, you can use your last will and testament to name the guardians of your children if you and your spouse pass away. If you're divorced, this is even more important.

POWER OF ATTORNEY FOR FINANCIAL MATTERS

As a financial planner, I tend to have a bias toward the importance of the financial power of attorney document. This is also referred to as a Durable General Power of Attorney. In this document, you can name the people who have a role in handling your financial issues. Typically, spouses name each other as their attorney-in-fact to handle their financial issues, but it doesn't have to be your spouse. I have worked with some clients where one of the kids was named as attorney-in-fact instead of their wife. Everybody's situation is different; it doesn't matter what others have done. Make this document reflect your wishes.

It is very important to keep the documents up to date. I had a married couple who were clients of mine, and the husband became bedridden. His wife was a nurse who left work to care for him. They had power of attorney forms, but those forms were more than a decade old. She needed to execute some transactions in his IRA account, but the financial institution challenged the power of attorney due to its age. She ultimately needed to meet with an attorney to draft an affidavit saying it was still valid.

A financial power of attorney is extremely important when it comes to two items I regularly deal with: qualified money (IRA accounts and retirement plans) and real estate. If a person becomes disabled, they can use the financial power of attorney document that named the person (or group of people) who should handle their financial affairs. If that doesn't happen, the ideal person may not be able to manage the investments as needed. The durable power of attorney provides the solution needed to enable accounts to be transferred from one custodian to another, if that is appropriate. It's an important document in handling financial assets and should not be overlooked.

A power of attorney document can be very helpful if you own real estate jointly and one of you becomes disabled. If a couple owns a large colonial home together and one spouse is disabled to the point of being in a wheelchair, the healthy spouse may say, "You know, this is just silly. We should sell this two-story colonial house and buy a ranch house, then modify it to be wheelchair-accessible." However, the healthy spouse won't be able to sell that property on their own. Without a power of attorney document in place, the healthy spouse would have to go through a probate conservatorship process. They'd need to go through a hearing and be appointed by the judge as the conservator in order to sell the property. It's an unnecessary process to go through and one that can be easily avoided by having this document in place in advance.

POWER OF ATTORNEY FOR HEALTHCARE MATTERS

Similar to a financial power of attorney form, a healthcare power of attorney form allows you to name people and assign responsibilities to them in the event you're unable to make decisions. In the healthcare power of attorney form, it's common (but not required) for the designated decision maker to be your spouse and then your kids as a backup. This document empowers your attorney-in-fact to decide on the preferred doctors, hospitals, and treatments that you would receive in an effort to manage your health issues.

If you're in a second marriage, a healthcare power of attorney form can be even more important. Do you want your second spouse to have authority over your health-care decisions, or would you rather give that authority to your children?

Think about the reality of that scenario: you're not doing well, you're in failing health, and you can't make your own healthcare decisions. Your second spouse and your children from your first marriage are at the hospital, and they're in complete disagreement and butting heads over what treatment you should get or not get. Instead of setting the stage for that stressful and problematic scenario, you could use a healthcare power of attorney to specify who should make decisions on your behalf. Hopefully, each side would respect your written instructions and not take it to probate court to battle it out.

LIVING WILLS

A living will, also known as an advanced health directive or healthcare proxy, handles the final stages of life, and this topic hits close to home for me. My dad passed away on January 11, 2005, and it still hits a nerve in me as if it was last month. My dad never wanted to be kept alive on life support. He saw his parents go through that, and he swore he would never go through that himself.

About six months prior to his passing, my dad was taken to the hospital from the nursing home. When it came time to make some decisions regarding my dad's treatment, the nurse came over in a not-so-professional way and blurted out, "Well, is there a living will?"

My mother and siblings were there with me at the hospital, and it caused some issues within the family when I popped up and said, "Yes, there is."

My brother and sister turned to me and were not happy. "What do you mean he has a living will?" There was a bit of a confrontation, and soon, my mom came walking over. My mom is about five feet tall, sweet as pie, and a phenomenal lady. "What's the commotion?" she asked.

"Well, Mom," I said, "they're unhappy that Dad had a living will."

Mom simply looked at them and said, "I do too." She then turned around and walked away, effectively ending that confrontation. My mother is a woman of few words, but those few words clarified how she felt about the importance of having a living will.

My parents did their planning before it was needed. They understood that their health could someday diminish to the point where they would no longer be able to lift a finger, blink an eye, or communicate in any way. They understood the importance of recording their decisions in a living will with the expectation that the family would follow through with those decisions. In my dad's case, he decided in advance that if he digressed into a non-communicative state, he did not want feeding tubes or a respirator. It was all spelled out in his living will.

To be clear, the advanced health directives within a living will are instructions for the medical community and the family. My dad wasn't instructing me to make decisions about feeding tubes. He had already made those decisions, and now it was our job as a family to make sure the medical community would comply with his instructions.

My dad's health declined further, and we followed his instructions to withhold treatment. He died three days later. If my dad hadn't put a living will in place, who knows how long he would have been kept alive artificially, on life support? It could have spanned many weeks or months, and that was not what my dad wanted.

I had a similar situation with my former mother-in-law, who had emergency surgery to correct a blocked intestinal tract. She never recovered and went onto life support.

Twelve days later, we had to make the same decision that was made for my dad.

Lastly, I had a cousin who was my age who also went onto life support after an operation. Like my former mother-in-law, she did not recover. Unlike my father, however, she did not have a living will in place. It was a very emotional time for the family because they were forced to decide what to do in terms of removing the artificial life support.

Having a living will in place can prevent problems that go well beyond finances. If there's any situation where family members are fighting and disagreeing about treatment decisions, the hospital will likely just step back and stay out of it. They might tell the family to figure it out and come back when they agree on a course of action, or recommend that they go to probate court to get a court order to settle the dispute. This is one of the many scenarios that underscore the importance of having your living will documents in place.

ATTORNEYS AND PLANNING: WHAT TO EXPECT

It's important to get these documents done in advance of needing them. If you become disabled, it may be too late.

When choosing your legal advisor, you'll want to work with an elder law or estate planning attorney who works solely in the arena of estate planning. In your first meeting, your attorney will get to know you and learn what's important to you. Then you'll discuss what you'd like to have happen when you pass away, and discuss who should serve as your attorney-in-fact in the event you become disabled.

Next, your legal advisor will lay out everything needed for your plan. The attorney I work with will also send out a letter to confirm everything that was discussed. If everything looks good and you're ready to begin, you'll pay a small deposit and the attorney will get started.

Documents are then drafted and reviewed during your next meeting with the attorney. If no changes are needed, the documents are signed, initialed, and notarized. At that point, your plan is in place. From start to finish, most of my clients finish their legal planning in four to six weeks.

I've met prospective clients who told me they'd been working on their last will and testament for over a year, and I think that is absurd. A last will and testament should not be that complicated. Additionally, I've met people who paid much more than necessary for their last will and testament. In some cases, people have paid more for their last will and testament than my attorney would charge for an entire plan (a trust, last will and testament, financial power of attorney, healthcare power of attorney, and advance health directives for both husband and wife).

This is one of the many reasons to get a referral from a trusted advisor who knows the costs and timelines of the attorney you'll be working with. I have also met with clients who have spent over a year "working" with an attorney to get just a last will and testament finalized. In my opinion, that is way, way too long for that process.

WHEN TO COMMUNICATE

It's helpful to get your planning done quickly while you're thinking about it. Once you've finished your planning, you should then tell your family about the documents and plans you've put in place. There are many good things that can come from this conversation. Even though the kids might not talk about it often, they typically are worried about their older parents and can feel better after a conversation about a living will and other legal plans. This conversation will also help to prevent problems down the line. Please keep in mind that your sons and daughters will typically not like to talk about Mom and Dad passing away, but persevere, as it is important to have that conversation.

You don't necessarily need to share your legal documents with your family, but at least let them know the documents are in place. Let them know the names of the advisors you're working with, including the attorney who drafted your documents and the location of your copies of those documents.

When it comes to the timing and frequency of communicating their plans to their family, I have clients on both ends of the spectrum. Some clients are proactive and highly communicative, holding annual family meetings to explain their plans and finances. On the other extreme, some people feel it's none of their kids' business and doesn't need to be addressed until the parents pass away. Everyone's situation is different, and you should communicate in the way that feels right for you. I do feel it's better to communicate your plans with your family whenever possible.

Early communication with your bank and financial institutions may also prove to be helpful. It's a good idea to take your power of attorney documents to your financial institutions to confirm the documents are fully understood, acceptable, and on record. It will be much easier for your attorney-in-fact to utilize their power of attorney if your financial institution has already reviewed and approved the documents.

For example, I've seen a large financial institution reject a power of attorney document because it didn't specifically state that the attorney-in-fact could change the beneficiary of an IRA. When my attorney heard about this, he was livid. He sent one of the longest emails I've ever seen, addressing each paragraph that gave the attorney-in-fact full power to manage every aspect of the account. That's the level of expertise you'll get by working with an attorney who is focused solely on elder law or estate planning. They know how to navigate these types of issues with financial institutions and custodians when it comes to the implementation of your legal documents and planning.

PEACE OF MIND

Whether it's for your parents or for yourself, having these legal documents in place will alleviate some of the stress of losing a loved one. While you might not be able to control the health of your parents, a living will can allow them to die peacefully and let nature take its course.

When people in their sixties tell me it's weird to think about dying, I tell them I understand, because I did this type of planning while I was in my forties. Indeed, it did feel a bit weird to imagine my own death, but once I finished my planning, I experienced the same relief I see in my clients when they finish their planning. I felt like a burden had been taken off my shoulders.

The importance of creating your legal documents cannot be understated. You could do everything else right, but if you mess up your legal documents, you will likely leave behind a stressful and complicated mess for your family. You want to make sure your documents are comprehensive, and part of a well-thought-out plan to protect your assets and make the transition as smooth as possible for your heirs.

Practicing Retirement

A few years ago, a married couple named Bob and Joan came into my office to discuss Bob's upcoming retirement. He had worked for a large public company for thirty-five years and felt it was time for him to start thinking about retirement. He was one of the fortunate few people who had a high-quality defined benefit pension plan. Based on his years of service to his company, he was set to receive 80 percent of his salary throughout his retirement years.

He loved working for his company and was grateful to be employed there, but he felt it was time to start enjoying his retirement. Before he would retire, however, Bob asked his company if he could work only four days a week, and the company approved his request.

Bob's reduced workweek and paycheck gave him the

opportunity to learn what it would be like to live on his retirement income. Four days of pay was the equivalent of his pension, and Bob wanted to practice retirement for a year, from an income standpoint. He and his wife Joan felt that if they could do that for one year without drawing money from the savings and assets they'd accumulated, they would be in great shape for Bob's full retirement. This exercise in practicing retirement worked quite well for them.

A lesson can be learned from Bob's story: you can practice your retirement. While you're still working, you can figure out what your retirement income will likely be. You can factor in your projected Social Security and pension income, add in any other source of income from investments or part-time employment and arrive at an estimated income for your retirement years. From there, you can begin to test that income against your budget.

If you need $4,000 per month for your lifestyle, but you only have three thousand dollars per month coming in from Social Security and your pension (if any), that's a gap of one thousand dollars per month. You'll then look to generate the additional one thousand dollars from your investments or perhaps a part-time job, or alternatively, you'll look to adjust your lifestyle to meet your budget. Similar to the way Bob practiced his retirement before he retired, you could see if you are able to live on three thousand dollars per month without needing the extra one thousand dollars from other sources. If you have expenses that will go away in retirement (like the costs of commuting to work), those expenses could be added to your budget while you're practicing retirement.

If you can practice retirement for a year without feeling the need to dip into your retirement savings, then you'll prove to yourself that you can actually retire. Running out of money is one of the biggest concerns shared by all my clients when discussing retirement, even if they have millions of dollars saved. This exercise helps everyone understand whether their fears are justified.

It might seem that the accumulation of one or two million dollars would be plenty for a person to feel comfortable in retirement, but people with larger incomes and investments often have a higher cost of living. They may have a membership at a premium country club, for example. This expense is an example of one that could be reduced or eliminated in retirement, but could also be increased in retirement, depending on how a person wishes to spend their time and money.

Whether it's the cost of golf or any other expense, just take a look at your overall expenses and determine which ones will carry forward into retirement. Then, even if you make thousands of dollars more than you need each month, practice living on that budget. Again, you can use the same income and expense sheet I use with my clients, by visiting www.masseyandassociates.com/expenses. It will only take you about fifteen minutes to determine your actual lifestyle expenses.

When looking at their projected expenses in retirement, many clients will say, "Well, I can cut many of these expenses out of my budget." However, my goal is for them to enjoy the lifestyle they've become accustomed to without needing to cut their budget. The challenge is to figure out how we can create the income and cash flow needed through a combination of Social Security, pensions, if any, and investment strategies. Then we'll move forward into retirement, and we'll adjust the plan as needed along the way.

LIFESTYLE CAN CHANGE IN RETIREMENT

Everyone's lifestyle is different, and it tends to change in retirement. When you're retired, you're going to have more time on your hands. Part of practicing retirement is to learn how to fill that time. For most people, their working hours and commuting time are over fifty hours per week. In addition to understanding the financial aspects of retirement, it's important to look at how you plan to spend your time.

What hobbies do you have currently? What hobbies do

you want to take up in the future? It's always best if you have hobbies before you get to retirement and have a good idea of which ones you enjoy the most. I like to golf on Saturdays and play billiards in the winter, and I know those are both hobbies I'll continue in retirement.

When retirees have no hobbies or personal plans in retirement, their mental and physical health tends to go downhill. They just sit on a rocking chair, or they sit on the couch and watch television. They're not as happy and tend to be grumpy, and it's unfortunate when I see it happening to a person in retirement. I always encourage my clients to pick hobbies that involve a circle of friends or family members, whether it's golf, playing cards, billiards, or whatever floats your boat. In my observation, the better your social network and range of activities, the better your retirement will be. My happiest retired clients are the busiest.

The irony of working with these very happy retirees is that they have less free time in retirement than they did when they were working, and it's harder for them to find time to set an appointment with me. When they were working, they would happily take some time away from work to come into my office for a meeting, but in retirement, they don't want to interrupt their fun activities. A client might have golf on Monday, a bridge game on Tuesday, billiards on Wednesday, bowling on Thursday, and so on.

Every day, they've got something fun planned, and it can be challenging to find a time that doesn't interrupt their enjoyable retirement schedule.

I also see a huge benefit for retired clients who watch their grandchildren and spend time with them regularly. I have two young grandchildren who are just phenomenal, and I love spending time with them. Whether it's every day or just once a week, it's a healthy and beneficial activity to spend time with grandchildren, and it can help their parents by reducing the astronomical costs of childcare.

Lastly, your lifestyle in retirement can be affected by the amount of money you wish to pass on to your family members or charities. Everyone has a different perspective on this decision. Many of my clients take the stance that if there's anything left for the children after the parents pass away, that's great, but the parents are going to focus on enjoying their retirement. Others really want to leave a significant inheritance for their children and/or grandchildren, and prioritize their retirement spending accordingly. In either situation, I can help them work toward their goal of maximizing their retirement income or maximizing the wealth that will be passed on to their heirs.

For all these reasons and more, practicing retirement is a good exercise and a cool idea. I highly recommend giving it a shot, seeing how you do, and then applying what you've learned to your retirement planning and the meetings you'll have with your financial advisor. You may be able to learn some aspects of retirement planning on your own, but I always suggest working with a Certified Financial Planner™ professional.

In the next chapter, I'll explain how to evaluate and choose the right advisor for you and your family so you can achieve and enjoy the best retirement imaginable.

Choosing the Right Advisor

Choosing the right advisor can be a simple task or a daunting one, depending on how difficult you want to make it. On my radio show, I speak often about the importance of choosing a Certified Financial Planner™ as your professional financial advisor. I've mentioned this several times throughout the book, because it's a level of expertise requiring college-level training. There are half a dozen courses, a ten-hour exam, and continuing education requirements to maintain this internationally recognized certification.

The exam that a CFP® is required to pass is on par with the examinations conducted for CPAs, doctors, and lawyers. It's a four-hour exam on a Friday afternoon, followed by a three-hour exam on Saturday morning, followed by another three hours of testing on Saturday afternoon. You must pass all three segments of the exam, or you'll be required to retake all three tests. When I took the exam in March of 2003, only 57% of all test takers passed the exam.[1] Those who pass the exam are then required to complete forty hours of continuing education every two years to maintain this credential.

The difficulty of achieving and maintaining the CFP® designation is what differentiates a CFP® from advisors who focus on only insurance products or investments. Those types of advisors are more likely to focus solely on investing dollars and growing assets. They don't have the range of credentials and education requirements of a CFP®, and it's a night-and-day difference when you sit with a CFP® to do your retirement planning. There is a requirement for a CFP® to have three years of actual work experience before they're allowed to publicize their CFP® designation, and you can feel confident they will truly understand the financial planning business.

COMMITMENT TO ONGOING EDUCATION

Continuing education is vital in the fast-changing world

---

1 "CFP® Examination Statistics", Certified Financial Planner Board of Standards, Inc., https://www.cfp.net/news-events/research-facts-figures/cfp-examination-statistics#Historical.

of financial planning, and you should assess an advisor's level of commitment to ongoing education. How many trainings do they go to each year? Are they forced to go to these trainings by their employer, or do they reach into their own pocket for the expense of conferences?

On average, I attend eight to ten conferences per year. That's a significant amount of training with highly advanced groups like the IRA-focused Ed Slott Organization. It's crucial to stay up-to-date with the many changing rules and tax issues regarding retirement plans to remain at the forefront of retirement planning.

I've been a member of the Ed Slott organization since 2010. Further, I'm a member of the Master Elite IRA Program, which has fewer than four hundred members.[2] Twice a year, we're required to complete two and a half days of training on 401(k) plans, 403B plans, and 457 plans, Simple IRAs, SEP IRAs, ROTH IRAs, Traditional IRAs, as well as the tax code changes relating to these plans.

Your financial planner should go above and beyond the minimum required training and should be experienced as an advisor and leader. How long have they been in the financial business? Are they a leader in the media?

---

2   "Elite IRA Consumer Group Consumer Page," IRAHelp.com, https://www.irahelp.com/about-ed-slotts-elite-ira-advisor-group.

I've had a successful radio program since 2006, and it's hard to stay on the radio for that long unless you're providing valuable insights and doing great things. In the *Providence Journal* 2017 Reader's Choice Awards, Massey & Associates, Inc. was voted one of the top three financial planning firms by readers of the newspaper. We are the only local advisor in the top three, as the other two finalists are national brands. We're very proud of this and feel there's a reason that the readers of the *Providence Journal* voted us to the top of the heap when it comes to financial planning. We are grateful for that recognition.

ASSESSING LEADERSHIP

Beyond ongoing education and media leadership, you should look for an advisor who is active in their professional associations and community. At one point, I belonged to three different professional associations, and when I asked to volunteer as the treasurer of the Financial Planning Association of Rhode Island, I decided to focus my efforts within that organization alone. I was voted onto the board and ultimately to each leadership position: treasurer, secretary, president-elect, president, and chairman. I dedicated over seven years to the association as a board member and found it to be personally rewarding. I remain an active member.

I believe a true financial professional should be making

an ongoing contribution to the larger community of financial planning. I'm very proud of our association and my involvement within it. We accomplished some wonderful things in our community and provided financial education to underserved people who benefitted greatly from it. Through my own experience, I understand the value of serving in leadership positions within a professional organization, and the extra effort it takes to make a significant contribution to your organization and community.

LIKEABILITY IS CRUCIAL

Beyond the CFP® designation, there are other important factors to consider when choosing an advisor. I find it helpful to approach this relationship the same way you'd approach dating a new person. You need to date them for a bit to determine whether you enjoy being around them. The first question you should answer is, "Do I like this person?" Hopefully, you're going to spend decades together, before and during retirement, and everything will be more enjoyable if you actually like your advisor.

This is also important from your advisor's perspective. When clients come into my office for the first time, I often get the compliment, "My goodness, we've met such nice people here." In reply, I bluntly and truthfully say, "Well, it's because we don't work with jerks." It's just that simple.

I actually had to ask a prospective client to leave my office only fifteen minutes after he came in. The gentleman was truly obnoxious, almost bragging about his poor treatment of tellers at his bank. I certainly didn't want anyone treating my staff like that, and I suggested that he should work with another advisor. "I'm sorry, sir," I told him. "We're not a good fit for you." He was dumbfounded. He had half a million dollars and expected that I would trip all over myself to serve him and accept any kind of behavior. Perhaps many advisors would be willing to work with him, but I only work with nice people. I know I bring a lot of value to the table, and when I see a client's name on my calendar, I want to have a smile on my face, and I hope that they will be smiling when they come in to visit. It's good for both the advisor and the client when they like each other.

SIMPLICITY IN COMMUNICATION

The next question to answer is, "Does this advisor speak to me in a manner that's simple and appropriate?" My favorite compliment to receive from clients is that I make things simple to understand. In one instance I mentioned earlier, a client came in to my office by himself for the first meeting, and I asked him to bring his wife to the next meeting.

"Well," he said, "she really doesn't like these kinds of meetings; she just lets me handle the finances."

Having heard this type of response many times, I replied, "Well, just humor me and bring her in. Have her come in for at least one meeting, and if she doesn't want to come back, that's perfectly fine."

Three meetings later, she was still coming in for every meeting. At the fourth meeting, I smiled and said to her, "I thought you didn't like coming to financial planning meetings?" She said, "You're the first person we've met with who makes it easy to understand what is going on."

I'm humbled and appreciative of a compliment like that because I work very hard to make things understandable and less complicated for my clients.

The financial services industry is complex, and some advisors prefer it to remain that way. I nearly walked out of a conference once when a speaker suggested purposely speaking over the heads of prospective clients. He claimed that clients' confusion would motivate them to meet with you, since the clients would feel uneducated on financial issues. I just shook my head and thought, "You have got to be kidding me."

You absolutely do not want to work with the type of advisor who constantly uses jargon and industry acronyms to confuse you. This recently happened to me during a complete technological meltdown in our office. In the same day, our computer systems, as well as our phone systems, went down. After frantically trying to get assistance for our phones, one company sent two young men to our office. They started speaking a mile a minute, using industry acronyms, and making zero sense to me.

I politely said, "Can you do me a favor and slow down a little bit? You're running through a lot of things here, and I have no idea what you're talking about."

They explained one or two items to me, but then they went right back into rapid-fire speaking and industry acronyms.

"All right, time out," I said. "I don't know what that means. You're using acronyms, and I don't have a clue what they mean. All I know is this: when I pick up the phone, I want to hear a dial tone when I want to call somebody. I couldn't care less about all the technology behind this. You can't speak to me in confusing acronyms and expect me to understand what you're doing."

In working with my clients, I do the opposite of what those two technicians did. I want people to understand their financial plan, their investments, and everything else I'm talking about. Simplicity in communication is crucial and should be heavily considered when choosing your financial advisor.

AVOID ONE-TRICK PONIES

As you look at different types of financial advisors, you want to avoid working with advisors who have only one product or investment type at their disposal. I call these types of advisors "one-trick ponies." They might be great people, but if they only sell insurance products or stock market investments, you'll be running the risk of allocating too much money into one type of asset.

As a Certified Financial Planner™, I'm able to access a broad range of products and choose what I feel is the best solution for you and your family. If your needs are best solved through an insurance product, I will bring that to the table. If it's best solved by a stock market investment, I'll bring that to the table. For many clients, the best solution is provided by a blend of products that provide the benefits of diversification.

It is important to diversify, as you will typically only be able to choose two of these three features in any financial product or investment: safety, liquidity, or growth potential. A simple example would be a bank savings account. This would offer safety and liquidity but little to no growth at today's interest rates. If you put all of your money there, you would simply go broke safely, due to the effects of inflation and taxation. Instead, you'd want to diversify into some products offering the feature of growth, to hopefully outpace inflation and strengthen your purchasing power in the future. For this reason, it's important to work with an advisor who is not pigeonholed into one category but can offer you a diverse array of financial products, investments, and retirement solutions.

FIND ADVANCED PLANNERS

In the wealth management formula referred to earlier in the book, I discussed the ideal combination of investment consulting, advanced planning, and relationship management. Serving clients in all three of these areas sets me apart from other advisors. Most advisors focus solely on the investment consulting piece. Their goal is simply to manage your investments and charge you a management fee of 1 percent (or more). At my firm, we go well beyond investment consulting and into the deeper, more valuable benefits of advanced planning.

In the realm of advanced planning, we help our clients enhance, protect, transfer, and gift their wealth. Roughly one-third of the clients I work with choose to make an impact on a charity with their wealth beyond their lifetime.

When focusing on wealth enhancement, we look at cash flow issues, income needs, and tax mitigation. In retirement, you want to minimize the taxation of your income as much as you can. Tax mitigation strategies may become increasingly important in the future, as I expect income taxes to rise in order to meet the expenditures of our federal debt and rising interest rates. I agree with the many economic and financial professionals who believe taxes will increase as it becomes difficult for our government to pay the interest on the federal debt.

Wealth protection is a critically important piece of advanced planning, and it will typically involve a combination of legal documents and services provided by a lawyer. Often, trusts are the tools chosen for this outcome, as trusts are effective in protecting assets and passing them on to your beneficiaries. For example, in the event your child is divorced in the future, a properly structured trust can protect the wealth you passed on to your family members by putting up a wall between your legacy to them and their divorcing spouse. This keeps the money with your child and not their ex-spouse (whom I refer to as the "outlaw"). This is one of the many scenarios that benefit from the proper protection of your wealth. You should pick an experienced attorney who is aware of this type of protection in a trust.

Wealth transfer issues are important to address with your financial planner. You want to ask and get answers to questions such as:

- What's the best strategy to pass assets to your family or causes?

- How do you maximize the amount of money that is passed on after tax?
- What's the best way to enhance or leverage the legacy you'd like to pass on to your family?

Some additional questions you should consider are:

- Do you want to provide a legacy for your children or family?
- If so, how much would you like them to receive?

Charitable giving is a priority for some of my clients, and it's an area of advanced planning you should expect from your financial advisor.

MANAGING RELATIONSHIPS

The relationship management component is the final element of the wealth management formula. This encompasses my focus on maintaining a great relationship with my clients, as well as maintaining great relationships with the other experts who bring valuable services to the table for my clients. An experienced financial planner will manage relationships and coordinate your planning with estate planning attorneys, elder law attorneys, CPAs, risk management professionals, and all other experts appropriate for your planning needs.

These professional relationships can save you time and money. For example, when was the last time you reviewed your property and casualty insurance with a different risk manager? If you've been with one firm for many years, that doesn't necessarily mean that you're getting the best deal. I've experienced this scenario myself, with an insurance brokerage I'd used for many years. One day I told my broker, "You know, it just seems like I'm paying a lot for this type of homeowners insurance."

"Oh," he replied, "would you like us to shop around for you?" There was a long pause on my end of the line, as I was shocked by this response. Shouldn't they always be doing that?

He shopped around for a better deal, and I saved hundreds of dollars on my homeowners insurance as a result of asking that question. Similarly, I ask clients to allow us to review everything that impacts their financial future. I look at their entire picture, not just investments or retirement income. Clients' insurance expenses should be evaluated to see if money can be saved or coverage improved, whether it's auto, home, life, disability, or any other form of insurance.

A comprehensive wealth manager will review every aspect of the wealth management formula: investment consulting, advanced planning, and relationship management.

That's what we do at Massey & Associates, Inc., and our new clients say that our Massey On Money™ Retirement Roadmap process sets us apart from other advisors they have met or worked with.

FURTHER INFORMATION AND RESOURCES

Thank you for reading my book, and I hope it has been helpful for you. If you have further questions about anything in the book, or are looking for a comprehensive advisor to be your retirement tour guide, please feel free to reach out to me at MasseyOnMoney.com or call my office directly at 401-333-8000.

According to many surveys, running out of money is the number one fear of retirees. It's the primary concern of the people I meet with who ask me if they'll have enough money to retire and whether they will outlive their retirement income. If you are like many retirees who are unsure as to whether your retirement plan will provide an adequate and lasting amount of income to support your lifestyle in retirement, please reach out to me. I'm happy to help you address those issues and concerns, and I'd be honored to sit with you and provide a complete analysis of your current situation and provide you with recommendations and strategies to assist to you and your family in achieving your retirement goals.

Thanks again for reading this book. I wish you a successful, blissful, and happy retirement.

About the Author

 JEFF MASSEY is president of Massey & Associates Inc., a wealth advisory firm specializing in retirement planning, investment management, asset management, tax planning, and estate planning. A Certified Financial Planner™ professional with more than two decades of experience, Jeff hosts the popular radio show Massey on Money™ and is a frequent speaker at financial conferences and seminars. Massey has held retirement planning classes at Rhode Island College and Bryant University. He is a US Army veteran and a lifelong Rhode Island resident who supports and volunteers for a number of charitable organizations, including the Special Olympics Summer Games, the Cumberland-Lincoln Boys and Girls Club, the RI Food Bank, and the Providence Rescue Mission.

Made in the USA
Middletown, DE
24 May 2019